AF556354

HYMENOPTERA
AND
BIOLOGICAL PEST CONTROL

By

Dr. T. V. Sathe

Department of Agrochemicals and Pest Management
Shivaji University
Kolhapur (Maharashtra)
(INDIA)

&

Dr. A.M. Bhosale

Department of Agrochemicals and Pest Management
Shivaji University
Kolhapur (Maharashtra)
(INDIA)

DISCOVERY PUBLISHING HOUSE PVT. LTD.

INDIA

Published by:

Namit Wasan

DISCOVERY PUBLISHING HOUSE PVT. LTD.

4383/4B, Ansari Road, Darya Ganj
New Delhi-110 002 (India)
Phone : +91-11-23279245, 43596064-65
Fax : +91-11-23253475
E-mail : discoverypublishinghouse@gmail.com
namitwasan9@gmail.com
sales@discoverypublishinggroup.com

website: www.discoverypublishinggroup.com

***First Edition:* 2017**

ISBN: 978-93-5056-849-1

Hymenoptera and Biological Pest Control

Printed at:
Infinity Imaging Systems
Delhi

Preface

Agriculture plays a very crucial role in sustainable development of a country by providing food and value added products. Indian agriculture encompasses much diversified geography and climatic conditions that enhance cultivation practices and cropping patterns. Several hybrid varieties were originated from India. But as compare to international level the predicted yield has not achieved so far because of severe infestation to agricultural crops through various insect pests. Hence, the appropriate pest management strategy to avoid the losses is the need of today's agriculture. The pest management tactics includes: chemical method, cultural method, mechanical method, genetic method etc. Out of which the chemical method through extreme use of pesticides can be usually accepted means of pest control as it shows quick knockdown effect, long residual action and easy to apply. But indiscriminate pesticide use resulted in to serious problems such as: environmental pollution, disturbance in eco-cycle, health hazards, pest resistance, pest resurgence, secondary pest outbreak, destruction to food webs and killing of beneficial organisms and insects, etc. Besides these the pesticide residue in soil, water, fruits and food can be reached above the maximum residue limit (MRL) prescribed by WHO and FAO.

The above facts clearly indicate that there is an extreme need to find out the solution for extensive pesticidal use and their crisis. The biocontrol method is the best solution for it. Biological pest control is regarded as most effective, economical, protective and eco-friendly method of pest control due to which it possesses prime place in the IPM strategy. Biocontrol methods are designed with parasitoids and predators. The parasitoids parasitize the pests and cause mortalities in them. Hymenoptera is parasitic order of insects which ranks first among all orders and the families like Braconidae, Ichneumonidae and Trichogrammatidae are extremely important from the view of parasitoid number and their biocontrol potential.

They are practically used against several insect pests. They destroy eggs, larvae, pupae and adults of the pest insects. Thus, hymenopterous parasitoids are very potential biopesticides scattered in nature and have greatest significance in pest management. The present work will provide information on Braconid and Ichneumonid parasitoids with respect to biology, rearing, host density, host specificity, host age selection, parasitoid longevity, behaviour and field efficacy, will be useful for mass rearing and utilizing parasitoids in biological control of insect pests on eco-friendly pest management strategies.

We hope that the present work will be helpful to students, teachers and researchers working in Biocontrol Institutes, Applied Entomology, pest management and life sciences.

Dr. T.V. Sathe
Dr. A.M. Bhosale

Contents

Introduction

The growing disparity in economic standard and social amenities between the village and the town needs to be bridged. This is possible by educational, cultural, economic, agricultural and industrial development (Sarkar *et al.* 2013). During the three quarters of this century India has made significant contribution in science and technology, which largely affecting the life and economic condition of people. Scientific research in capitalist countries has made very remarkable progress mainly due to large investments made by industries for utilizing manpower and talent in science and technology. Industrialization should spread rapidly in agricultural sector for development of agriculture and related industries. The impressive spectacular achievements in agriculture, industry, space programme and social science that have been made in the socialist country during the short period of 3 to 4 decades are mainly due to enormous drive for universal education, particularly science education (Sarkar *et al.* 2013).

According to Directorate of Economics and Statistics (2001), China has shown remarkable success in solving two basic economic problems of food and employment. "About 40 to 60 per cent people in India are still illiterate and on the economic front they had plunged from no 51 to 105 in the list; even extremely backward countries in Africa which won freedom after India, have gone ahead in the name of socialism." After 30 years of freedom we have achieved and progressed less in comparison to what the USSR did in not more than 4 decades after liberation from the Czarist rule.

Science is the determining factor in economic and cultural life. Hence, science needs a massive approach for the economic development. In India where, more than 75 per cent people live on agricultural occupation should develop export trade on cereals and other farm products in addition to their normal requirements (Sarkar *et al.* 2013).

Agriculture is mainstay for our villagers; increase in agricultural productivity is essential for rural economy for which research in the new prospective is all that we visualize towards self-sufficiency in food, export of farm products and agricultural oriented jobs for the rural people (Sarkar *et al.* 2013). Among several agro-based industries silk industry is an important one which can provide employment to both men in the field and women in the house, should be encouraged at large extent in India.

Agriculture is most crucial part of Indian economy which provides livelihood to about 70 per cent of the population of India (Paroda, 1993). Importance of agricultural sciences in national planning and development is recognized by all advanced countries (West, 2012). In fact, development of any country is dependent on technological improvement including agricultural sector. Agriculture supplies basic requirements for the existence of human beings and for the development of agro-based industries. Fluctuations in the prices of agricultural commodities are dependent on the crop yield, which is based on application of improved agronomic practices, environmental factors and mostly efficient management of pests and diseases.

According to Directorate of Economics and Statistics (2001), agriculture trade is contributing 40-50 per cent of the total foreign exchange and plays very crucial role in Indian export. India (Fig. 1.1) is having extremely diversified climatic conditions and hence different cropping patterns and there by pest control problems do arise.

Maharashtra (Fig. 1.2) is one of the most industrialized, urbanized and agriculturally sound state in India. Its economy is undoubtedly dependent on agriculture sector (Sawant *et al.* 1999). Western Maharashtra is belt of advanced agriculture, floriculture and horticulture practices specially; Kolhapur, Sangli and Satara districts of Western Maharashtra (Fig. 1.3) are advanced states in above farming having conductive environment and high biodiversity. Hence, the present topic has great relevance.

The cropping pattern (Fig. 1.4) of Maharashtra is dominated by food grains and other several types of crops (FAO, 2013). The cereals and pulses crops have major importance as they are used in daily human diet which fulfills the nutritional requirements.

In the year 2012, India was at fourth position in the production of Sorghum with the production of 6000 MT contributing 11.2 per cent of the total world sorghum production. Indian scientist developed first hybrids in several crops like: cereals, cotton, castor, etc.

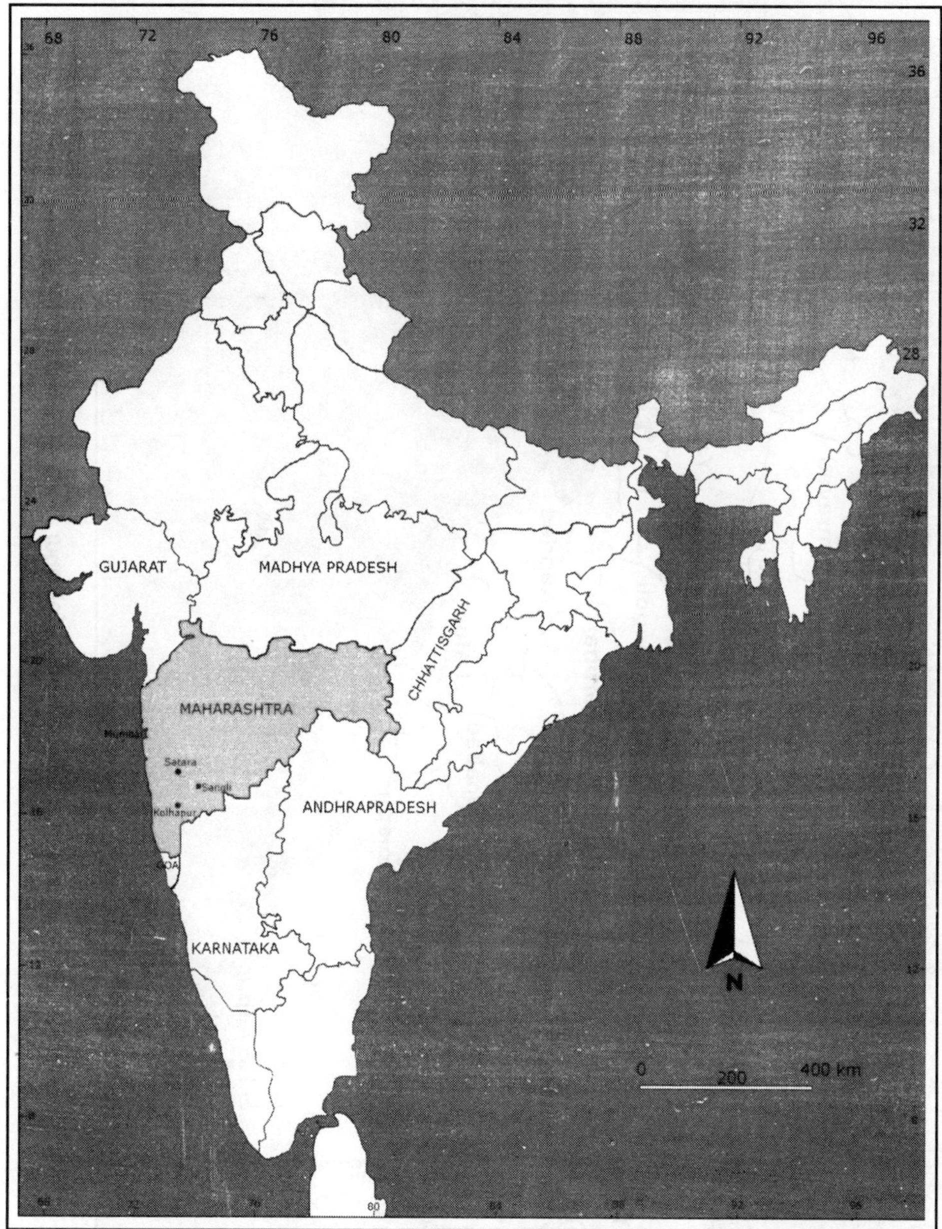

Fig. 1.1: **Map of India Showing Maharashtra (Study Area)**

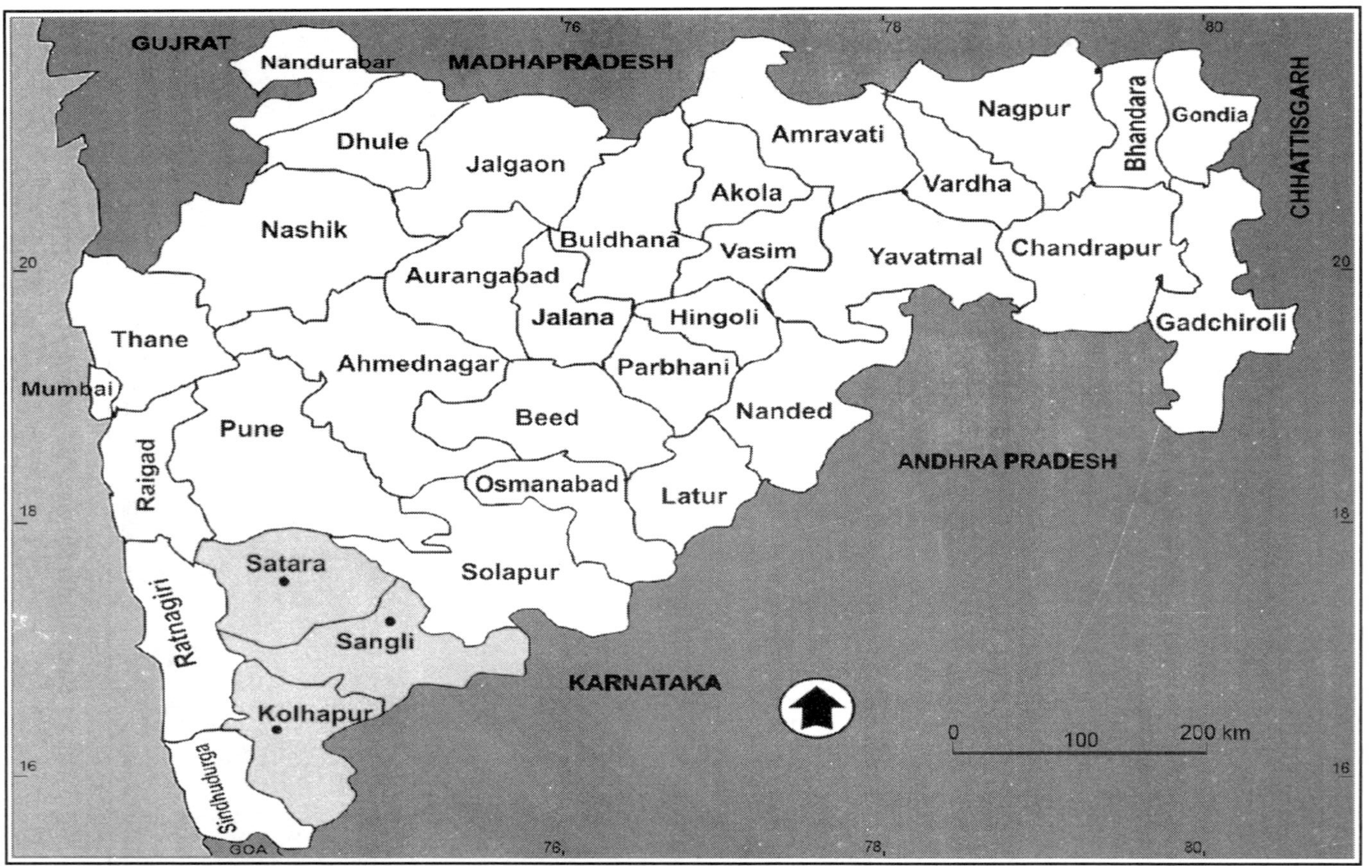

Fig. 1.2: **Map of Maharashtra Showing Districts Kolhapur, Sangli and Satara (Study Area)**

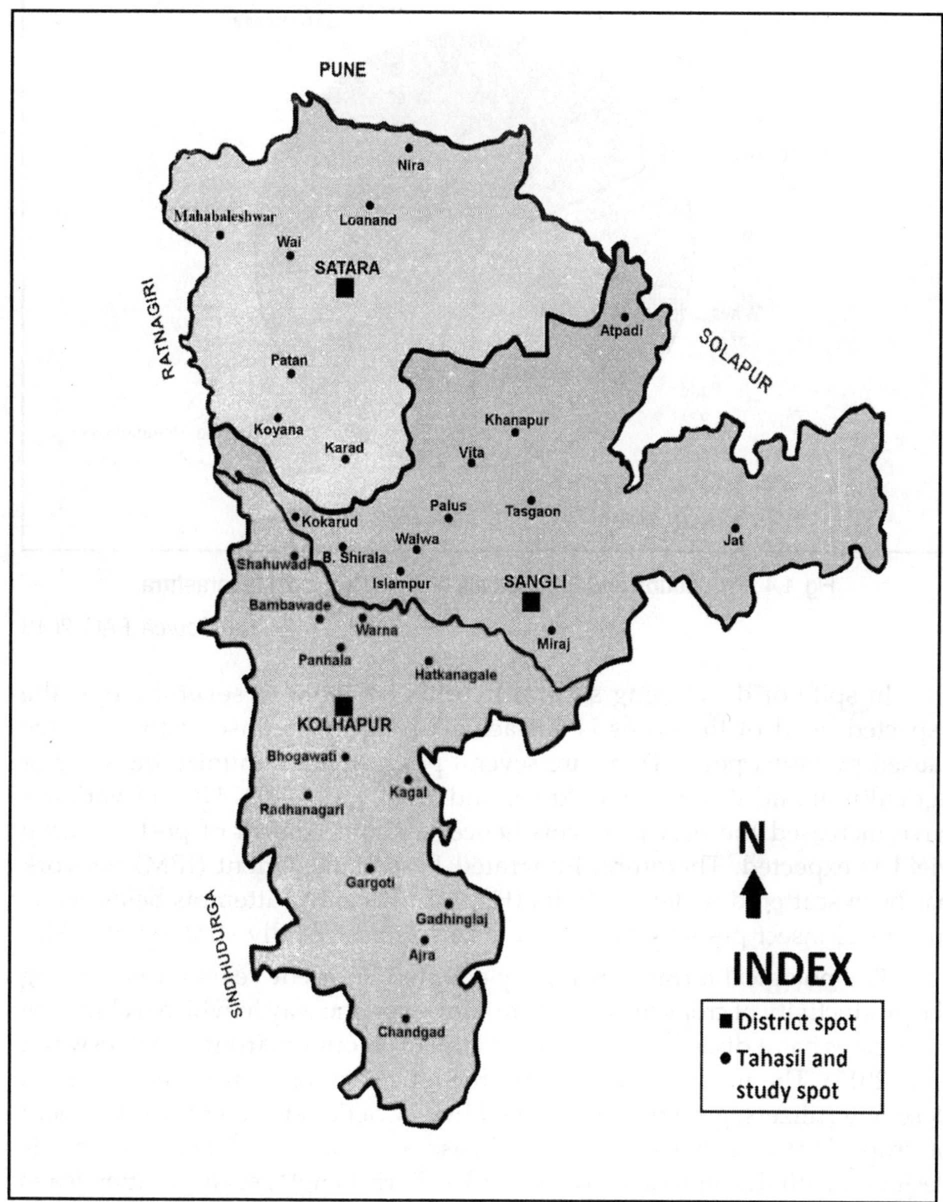

Fig. 1.3: **Map of Districts Kolhapur, Sangli and Satara Showing Study Spots**

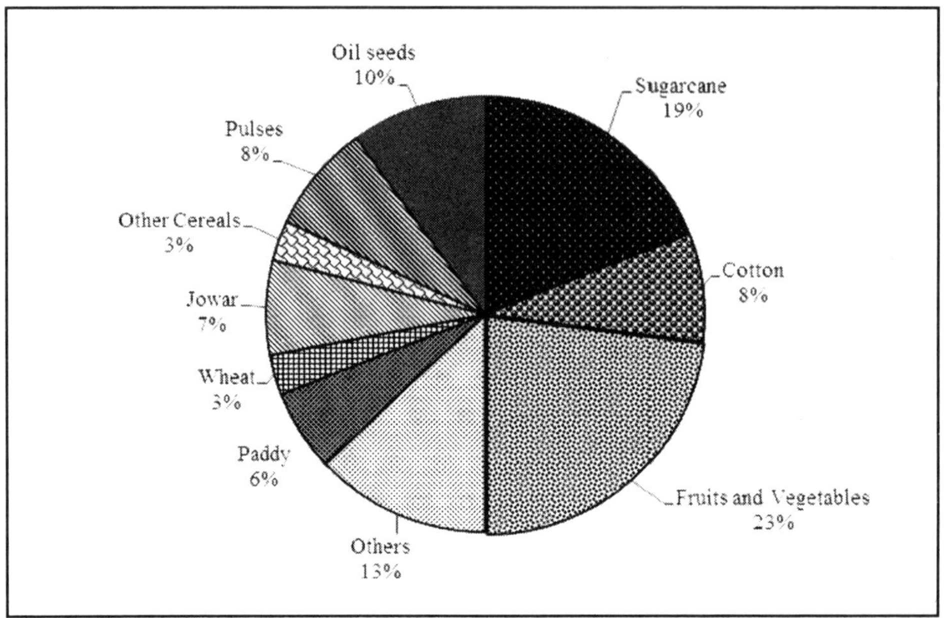

Fig. 1.4 : **Production and Productivity of Field Crops of Maharashtra**

**Source*: FAO, 2013

In spite of developing several hybrids by India in several crops, the expected yield of the crops is not achieved so far because of the damage caused by insect pests. There are several pests which minimize the yield of agricultural and other crops (Atwal and Dhaliwal, 2002). Hybrid varieties have increased the pest problems hence, without control of pests no crop yield is expected. Therefore, Integrated Pest Management (IPM) network has been scattered widely in India (Fig. 1.5). Recently, attempts being made to control insect pests by biological means as ecofriendly strategy of IPM.

Technological farming is widely adopted in recent years for enhancing the productivity of crops in agriculture. However, the way in which technology progresses has a disastrously negative impact on our environment (Goswami *et al.* 2013). The new technology and the efficiency of its use, such as: high dose of fertilizers, growing of high yielding varieties etc., increased the yield of crop plants but boosted pest and disease problems. Hence, control is designed with the high doses of pesticides. Surprisingly, such situation leads to the drastic increase in the population of pests which is the self-creating phenomenon by man. Therefore, there is need to develop ideal methods or integrated pest management method for pest control. Sundarmurthy and Chitra (1984) developed the pest management model (Fig. 1.6) which is helpful for minimizing the use of pesticides for control of insect pests. FAO (2013) reported the entomological activities in cropping system of India (Fig. 1.7).

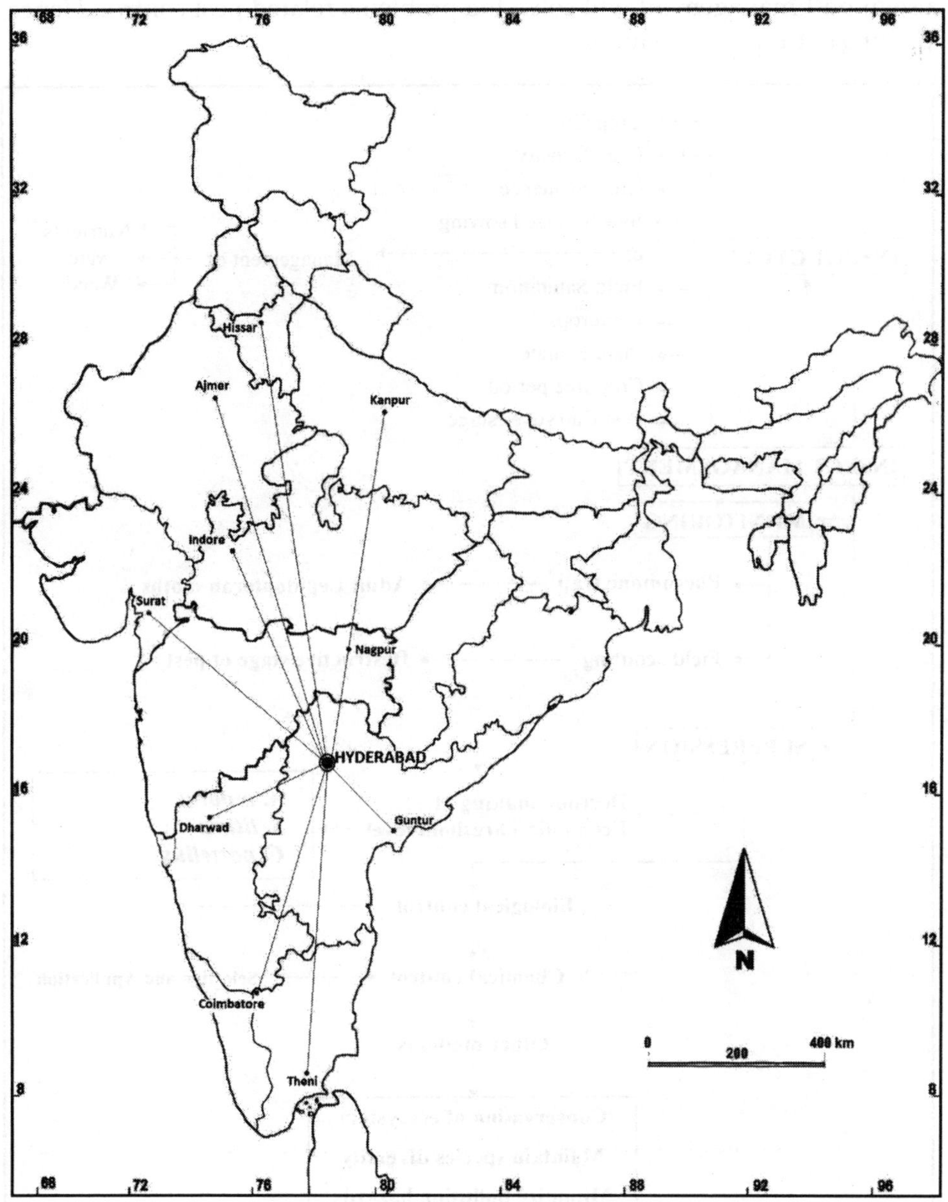

Fig. 1.5: **Integrated Pest Management Network of India**

**Source*: Sathe and Margaj, 2001

Since hymenopterous parasitoids are very good biocontrol agents of several insect pests and are biopesticides scattered in nature, their judicious use in pest management will solve the problems related pest control. Hence, the present topic was chosen.

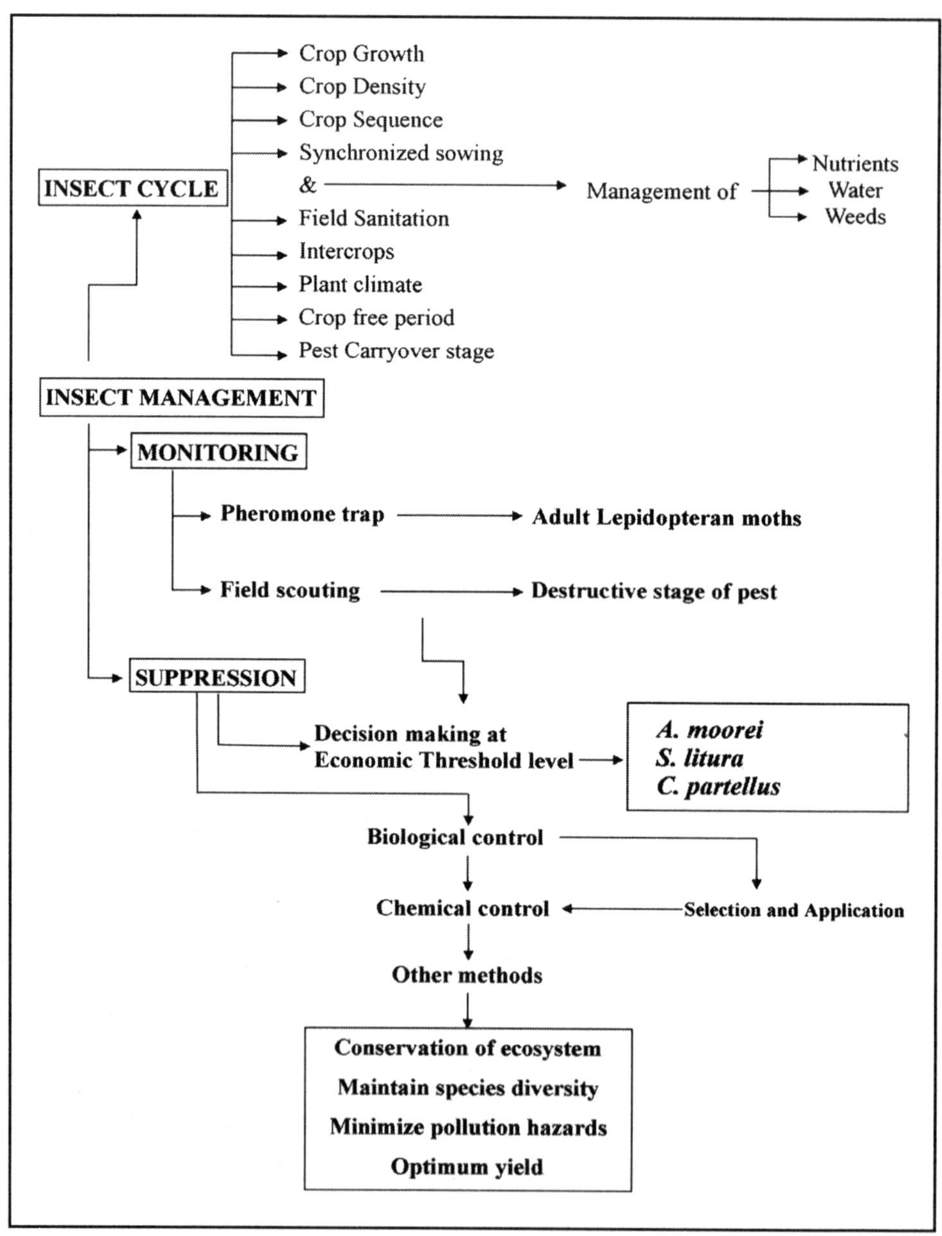

Fig. 1.6: **Pest Management Model for Agricultural Crops**

**Source* Sundarmurthy and Chitra, 1984

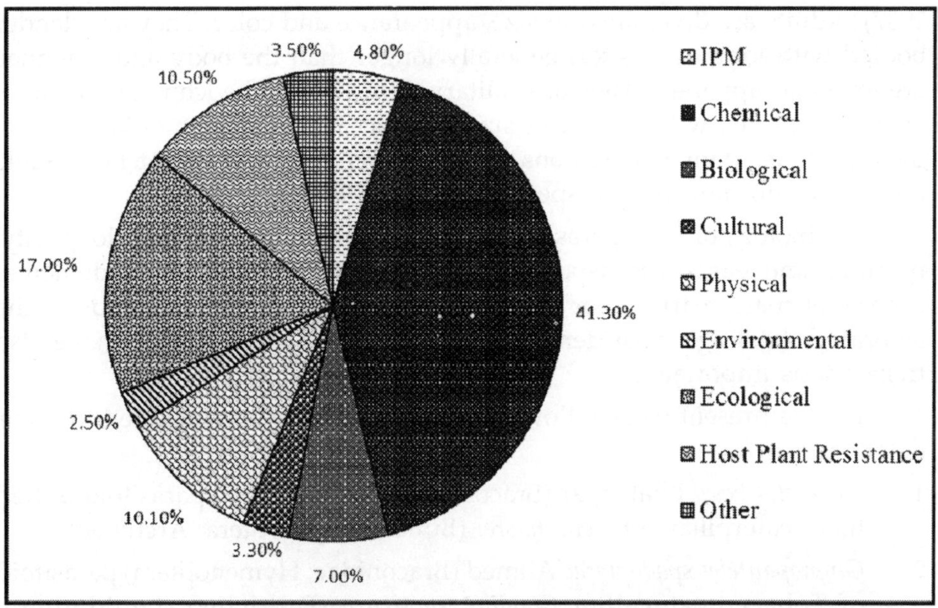

Fig. 1.7: **Entomological Research Activities in Cropping System of India**

**Source*: FAO, 2013

The hymenopteran parasitic wasps are beneficial as biocontrol agents of insect pests and incapable of stinging humans. Such wasps use their sting as the ovipositor for egg laying inside the host body. Parasitic wasps consist of the large and most potent group of natural enemies of insect pests. It has been assumed that almost every insect species which infest plants is attacked by one or more parasitoid species (Townes, 1969; Coppel and Martins, 1977). Parasitoid wasps vary in their size, biology, host, parasitism, etc. The parasitoids are the pest population regulatory factors.

In the present study both braconids and ichneumonid have been selected for their detail studies. Braconidae is a large group of parasitic insects which contain about 40,000 species described all over the world (Mason, 1986). Most braconids are small wasps, generally black or brown in color, but some shows yellow, orange or red markings. They have long and clearly visible antennae and the ovipositor may also be long and readily noticeable. The lifespan of most braconids is comparatively short as compare to ichneumons. The second recurrent vein is absent or sometimes single vein may present whereas, the ichneumonid parasitoids having two recurrent veins. Most braconids are primary parasitoids of the insect pests, particularly they parasitizes the larval stages of agricultural pests.

Ichneumonidae family constitutes the largest groups of parasitoids containing about 60,000 described species from all over the world (Gupta,

1987). Adults are diversified in size, appearance and color. They are slender bodied with long ovipositor, generally longer than the body and antennae are long and apparent. They are solitary parasitoids. The ichneumon wasps are more familiar with their large size which is about three times longer than the braconids. Many Ichneumons prefer different pest insects as a host, while others are enormously host specific (Idris and Hainidh, 2003).

The biology of these parasitoids with their lifecycle, behaviour, longevity, nutrition and parasitism aspects required special attention as fundamental aspects of mass rearing. For enhancing mass rearing of parasitoids in the laboratory host age, host density, host specificity and fecundity have also tremendous importance.

For the present work following parasitoids have been selected for their detail studies

1. *Apanteles bosei* Bhatnagar (Braconidae: Hymenoptera) parasitoid of Red hairy caterpillar *Amsacta moorei* (Butler) (Lepidoptera: Arctiidae).
2. *Glyptapanteles spodopterae* Ahmed (Braconidae: Hymenoptera) parasitoid of Tobacco caterpillar *Spodoptera litura* (Fabricius) (Lepidoptera: Noctuidae).
3. *Xanthopimpla pedator* Fabricius (Ichneumonidae: Hymenoptera) parasitoid of Jowar stem borer *Chilo partellus* Swinhoe (Lepidoptera: Pyralididae).

Review of Literature

Nutritional Requirement

The review of literature indicated that at national and international senario several workers have investigated nutritional requirements for parasitic hymenoptera including: braconids and ichneumonids. Ahmed and Ghulamullah (1941), have studied the nutritional requirement of parasitoids of spotted bollworms. Cherian and Narayanswami (1942) reported the longevity of *Microbracon chilonis* Viereck, the larval parasitoid of *Chilo zonellus* ------ (Swin.). Similarly, the parasitoid adult longevity of *Earias* sp., the spotted boll worms of cotton crop was studied by Khan and Verma (1945). Hidaka (1965), studied the parasitoids and predators associated with rice stem borer with their nutritional requirement and ecological peculiarities from Japan. Likely, Kajita and Drake (1969) analyzed the nutritional requirement of lepidopteran stem borer *Chilo suppressalis* (Walker) and their associated parasitoids *Cotesia flavipes* (Cameron) and *Cotesia chilonis* Munakata. Broodryk (1969), analyzed the nutritional requirement of *Chelonus curvimaculatus* Cameron. Oatman *et al.* (1969), studied the longevity of *Orgillus lepidus* Muesebake, an internal larval braconid parasitoid of potato tuber worm. Similarly, Hamid *et al.* (1970), reported the longevity of an ichneumonid parasitoid, *Brachycoryphus nursei* (Cameron), from Pakistan. Whereas, nutritional requirement of *Apanteles dingus* Muesebek, the braconid parasitoid of tomato pinworm was analyzed by Cardona and Oatman (1971). Likely, Odebiyi and Oatman (1972) studied the longevity of *Agathis gibbosa* (Say), a braconid parasitoid of potato tuber worm. While, Sato (1975) conducted experiments to study nutritional requirement of *Cotesia glomerotus* (Linn.) on

Pieris repae crucivora Biosduval caterpillars he gave an artificial diet to the host larvae. Likewise, Calkins and Suttar (1976) and House (1977), studied the longevity in *Apannteles millitaris* Wals and *Apannteles* sp. Sathe and Nikam (1983) analyzed adult longevity of *C. flavipes*, by providing different types of food. Somchoudhary and Dutt (1988) studied the nutritional demand of two *Trichogramma* species whereas, Sathe and Bhosale (1996) reported the nutritional requirement of adults of *Apanteles creatonoti* Viereck, a parasitoid of the *Spilosoma obliqua* (Walk). Canas and Robert (1998) applied sugar solution on maize crop as nutrition to parasitoids of fall armyworm. In 2001, Sathe and Margaj investigated the nutritional requirements for *Apanteles earterus* Wilkinson, *Apanteles pectinophorae* Ferr. and *Apanteles pusaensis* Lal., all braconids. Harvey *et al.* (2003), studied the effect of different dietary sugars and honey on longevity in *Lysibia nana* Gravenhorst and Gelis *agilis* Fab. as hyperparasitoids of *Cotesia glomerata* L.

Mating and Oviposition Behaviour

The behavioural studies of parasitoids like: mating and oviposition have been attempted by several workers from the world. Seither and Notzl (1925), Genieys (1925), Fink (1926), Matthews (1969; 1974), Leong and Oatman (1968), Broodryk (1969), Biliotti and Daumal (1969), Harbo and Kraft (1969), Kajita and Drake (1969), Oatman *et al.* (1969), Cole (1970), Lewis (1970), Cardona and Oatman (1971), Odebiyi and Oatman (1972), Vinson (1972), Oatman and Platner (1974), Dowell and Horn (1975), Quednau and Guevremont (1975), Lyons (1976), Weseloh (1981), Jackson (1978), van den Assem (1986), Battaglia *et al.* (2002), Romani *et al.* (2008), Benelli *et al.* (2012) etc., have contributed on mating behaviour in parasitic hymenoptera at global scenario. While, from India mating and oviposition in parasitic hymenoptera have been reported by Sathe and Nikam (1983, 1984), Sathe and Bhosale (1996), Sathe and Margaj (1996, 2001). In addition, Ayyar and Narayanswami (1940) studied the mating behaviour in *Spathius vumeficus* Wilk., a parasitoid of *Pempheres affinis* Faust from south Indian states. Nishida (1956) studied oviposition behaviour of *Opius fletcheri* Silvestri, a parasite of the melon fruit fly. Nobel and Graham (1966) demonstrated the mating behaviour in *Campoletis perdistinctus* (Viereck). Matthews (1974) reported the oviposition and mating behaviour in some braconid parasitoids. Leong and Oatman (1968) studied the oviposition and mating behaviour in an ichneumon parasitoid, *Campoplex haywardi* Blanchard which is primary parasitoid of potato tuber worm. The oviposition and mating behaviour of *Phanerotoma flavitestacea* Fischer, the braconid parasitoid was analyzed by Biliotti and Daumal (1969). Similarly, Harbo and Kraft (1969) studied the mating behaviour of *Phanerotoma toreutae* Caltagirone, the larval parasitoid of pine cone moth *Laspeyresia torenta* Walsh. Cole (1970) observed the searching of parasitoid males for females to mate in *Phaeogenes ivisor* (Viereck) and *Apanteles medicanginis* Cameron. Vinson (1972) reported the behavioural pattern of two parasitoid species of tobacco budworm. Likely, a parasitoid of potato tuber worm *Temelucha* sp., and *Platensis* sp., (Ichneumonidae) was studied with respect to mating and oviposition behaviour by Oatman and Platner (1974). Dowell and Horn (1975) explained the mating behaviour of *Bathyplectes curculionis* (Thomson), an ichneumon parasitoid of alfalfa weevil *Hypera postica* (Gyllenhal). Similarly, Quednau and Guevremont (1975) observed the oviposition and mating behaviour in *Priopoda nigricollis* (Thos.) (Ichneumonidae) against leaf miner *Fenusa pusilla* (Linn.). Lyons (1976) recorded mating ability of parasitoid, *Neodiprion sertifer* (Geoffroy) through their in-vitro mass rearing while, Waseloh (1977) found details of mating behaviour of *Cotesia* (=*Apanteles*) *melanoscelus* Ratzeburg, the braconid parasitoid of gypsy moth *Lymantria dispar* (Linn.). From India, Sathe and Nikam (1983, 1984) studied mating and oviposition in *Diadegma trichoptilus* (Cameron), *Diadegma argenteopilosa* (Cameron), *Campoletis chlorideae* Uchida, *Cotesia orientalis* Chalikwar and Nikam and *Cotesia diurnii* R.&N. (Sathe, 1990). Similarly, Sathe and Bhoje (1996) studied the oviposition behaviour of *Apanteles oblique* Wilkinson on the lepidopterous pest *Spilosoma obliqua* (Walker). Steiner *et al.* (2010), reported antennal courtship and functional morphology of tyloids in the *Syrphoctonus tarsatorius* (Panzer), an ichneumon parasitoid of agricultural pests.

Reproductive Potential (Host specificity, Host density and Host age selection)

Several workers have worked on reproductive potential of parasitic hymenoptera. Thrope and Jones (1937) reported the olfactory conditions in parasitic insects and their relation for host selection by the parasitoids. Barlett (1953) studied a tectile oviposition stimulus for in-vitro rearing of *Macrocentrus ancylivorus* Rohwer on an unnatural host and the host selection of the parasitoid for mass culture. Tawfik (1975) reported the host-parasitoid interaction and host specificity of the braconid parasitoid *Cotesia glomeratus* L. Lingren *et al.* (1970), Lingren and Nobel (1972) conducted an experiments for selection of optimum host density and host age preference by the parasitoid *Campoletis perdistinctus* (Viereck) against some noctuid larvae. Similarly, Lewis (1970) studied the species and different instars of *Heliothis* caterpillars for parasitism by *Microlitis croceipes* (Cresson). Azuma and Kitano (1971) analyzed experimentally the parasitism of *C. glomeratus* on the caterpillars of *Pieris melete* Menetries and reported the host age selection and host density preference by the parasitoids. Drooz and Fedde (1972) described the host age selection of *Monodontomerus dentipes* (Dalman) whereas, Calvert (1973) reported host preference of *Monoctonus paulensis* (Ashmead) for the host selection by the parasitoids. Oatman and Platner (1974) conducted experiments for the host age and host density selections on *Temelucha* sp and *Platensis* sp. Vinson (1975) estimated the biochemical evaluation between parasitoids and hosts which favours the host selection and maximum parasitization. Thurston and Postely (1978) studied the effect of host age of *Manduca sexta* (Linn.) on the rate of development of parasitoid *Cotesia congregates* (Say). Similarly, Jackson *et al.* (1979) illustrated the parasitization by *Chelonus blackburni* Cameron (Braconidae), on six lepidopteran cotton pests. Likely, Hopper and King (1984) investigated host age preferences of *M. croceipes* for different instars of *Heliothis zea* (Boddie). Somchoudhary and Dutt (1988) conducted the study on host and host age phenomenon of two *Trichogramma* species along with their nutritional demand. At the national senario, Sathe and Shanthakumar (1992) conducted the host specificity study in *C. chlorideae* whereas host density of *A. creatonoti* on the *S. obliqua* was studied by Sathe and Bhosale (1996). Sathe and Margaj (2001) also studied the host density, host specificity and host age selection by the three braconid parasitoids namely, *A. earterus*, *A. pectinophorae* and *A. pusaensis*, all braconids. Dung *et al.* (2011) studied the host density of parasitoid *Xanthopimpla punctata* Fabricius on soybean leaf folder *Omiodes indicata* (Fabricius). Sathe (1991), analyzed the fecundity and life table studies in braconid parasitoid *Glyptapanteles malshri* S and I, in *Plutella xylostella* (Linn.). Onagbola *et al.* (2007), reported fecundity and progeny sex-ratio of *Pteromalus cerealellae* (Ashmead) in relation to hosts provided.

Field Efficacy

As regards to field efficacy of parasitoids Kajita and Drake (1969) conducted the trials for lepidopteran stem borer *Chillo suppressalis* Walker with their associated parasitoids *C. chilonis* and *C. flavipes*. Barnes *et al.* (1976) studied the introduction, mass release of parasitoids for control of pine woolly aphid. Lewis and Gross (1989) conducted field experiment through comparative study of performance of parasitoids *M. croceipes* and *Cardiochiles nigriceps* Viereck which were larval parasitoid of *Heliothis* sp. The parasitoids were released in the field at various densities and varied from crop to crop and found to be efficient in minimizing the pest population. Similarly, Wanga *et al.* (2014) conducted an experiment to control the pests associated with maize crop by mass rearing and field release of *Trichogramma* species from Xinjiang region of China (Ma *et al.* 2000). Likewise, Li *et al.* (2006) tried to control the pest population of *H. armigera* from Xinjiang region of China through the field release of *Microplitis mediator* (Haliday) parasitoid. Resently, Abd-Rabou (2011) investigated the biological control of green shield scale *Pulvinaria psidii* Maskell on guava trees in Egypt through *Coccophagus scutellaris* (Dalman) whereas, Tilley *et al.* (2011) tested the braconid parasitoid *Aphaereta debilitata* Morley against shore fly *Scatella tenuicosta* Collin under the glass house. Recently Sathe (2014), contributed on recent trends in biological pest control. Similarly, Sathe (2015), also contributed the work on biological control through Ichneumonids.

Review of literature indicates that very little attention is paid on Indian parasitic hymenoptera and their utility except the work of Sathe and his coworkers. Hence, there is tremendous scope to enlighten the ichneumonid and braconid parasitoids for their diversity, reproductive potential and utility in biological pest control programmes.

Collection, Preservation and Rearing of Biocontrol Agents and Pests

Biological pest control may adversely affect due to slight change in mass rearing technique of biocontrol agents. Hence, appropriate techniques and favorable environment in the laboratory enhances the mass culture of parasitoids and their hosts. Thus, for rearing of parasitoids and hosts following materials and methods were employed.

MATERIALS

Glass Cages (Plate 1, Fig. 3.1-I and 3.1-II)

The two types of glass cages (size 25×25×30 cm) were used for rearing of hosts and their parasitoids. The cages were made up of wooden base with quadrangular shape and glass walls on all four sides in type I (Fig. 3.1-I) and with the door of cage with sliding glass window. While, in the type II (Fig. 3.1-II), one side of cage was provided with muslin cloth sleeve, as a door and for handling of pest species. Host specificity, host age selection, mass culture of hosts and parasitoids etc., were studied with the help of such glass cages.

Plastic Containers (Plate 1, Fig. 3.2 and 3.3)

Different size of plastic containers (4×4, 5×5, 5×6, 6.5×8cm) were used for individual rearing of parasitoids and their hosts. All plastic containers along with their lids were perforated for ventilation which minimized the suffocation of pests and parasitoids.

Plate - 1 (Figs. 1-3) **Insect rearing materials:** Fig. 3.1: **Rearing cages (Type - I: Rearing cage with glass) (Type - II: Rearing cage with sleeve),** Fig. 3.2: **Small plastic containers,** Fig. 3.3: **Large plastic containers**

Glass Troughs (Plate 2, Fig. 3.4)

The glass troughs were used for keeping and rearing the host larvae which were collected from the field for parasitoid emergence. The glass troughs were covered with muslin cloth to avoid escape of hosts and parasitoids. They are of two sizes 9×12cm and 20×25cm (Diameter×Height).

Test Tubes (Plate 2, Fig. 3.5)

Adult longevity and mating behaviour of parasitoids were observed by exposing them in test tube of size 15×2, 19×2.5, 20×2.8cm (Length ×Diameter). The test tubes were also used for handling of parasitoids during the study and for better to keep them separate for mating behaviour experiment.

Specimen Tubes (Plate 2, Fig. 3.6)

The specimen tubes were used for storing of parasitoids and cocoons. The open end of specimen tube was closed with the help of cotton or muslin cloth for maintaining ventilation. Specimen tubes (size 5cm and 10cm height, 2cm diameter) with lid on top were also used for storing of parasitoid adults in 70 per cent alcohol.

Petri Dishes (Plate 2, Fig. 3.7)

The petri dishes were used for keeping the eggs and early instar caterpillars for observing the parasitoid emergence. Petri dishes (size 9cm and 18.5cm diameter) also used for study of oviposition behaviour of parasitoids.

Digital Camera (Plate 3, Fig. 3.8)

The photography was made with the help of Sony Cyber-shot digital camera of 12.1 mega pixel with 4X optical zoom. The immature stages of parasitoids were captured by placing the camera on the top of microscope. The photographs were made with 10 times more resolution than normal photographs.

Microscope (Plate 3, Fig. 3.9)

The immature stages and small parasitoid species were observed and snapped by placing the camera on eyepiece of microscope.

Insect Collecting Net (Plate 3, Fig. 3.10)

The insect collecting net was used for collecting the pests and parasitoid species from the field.

Camel Hair Brush (Plate 3, Fig. 3.11)

The hair brush No. 5-10 was more useful for handling of small host caterpillars, eggs of hosts for transfer from one container to another without damage.

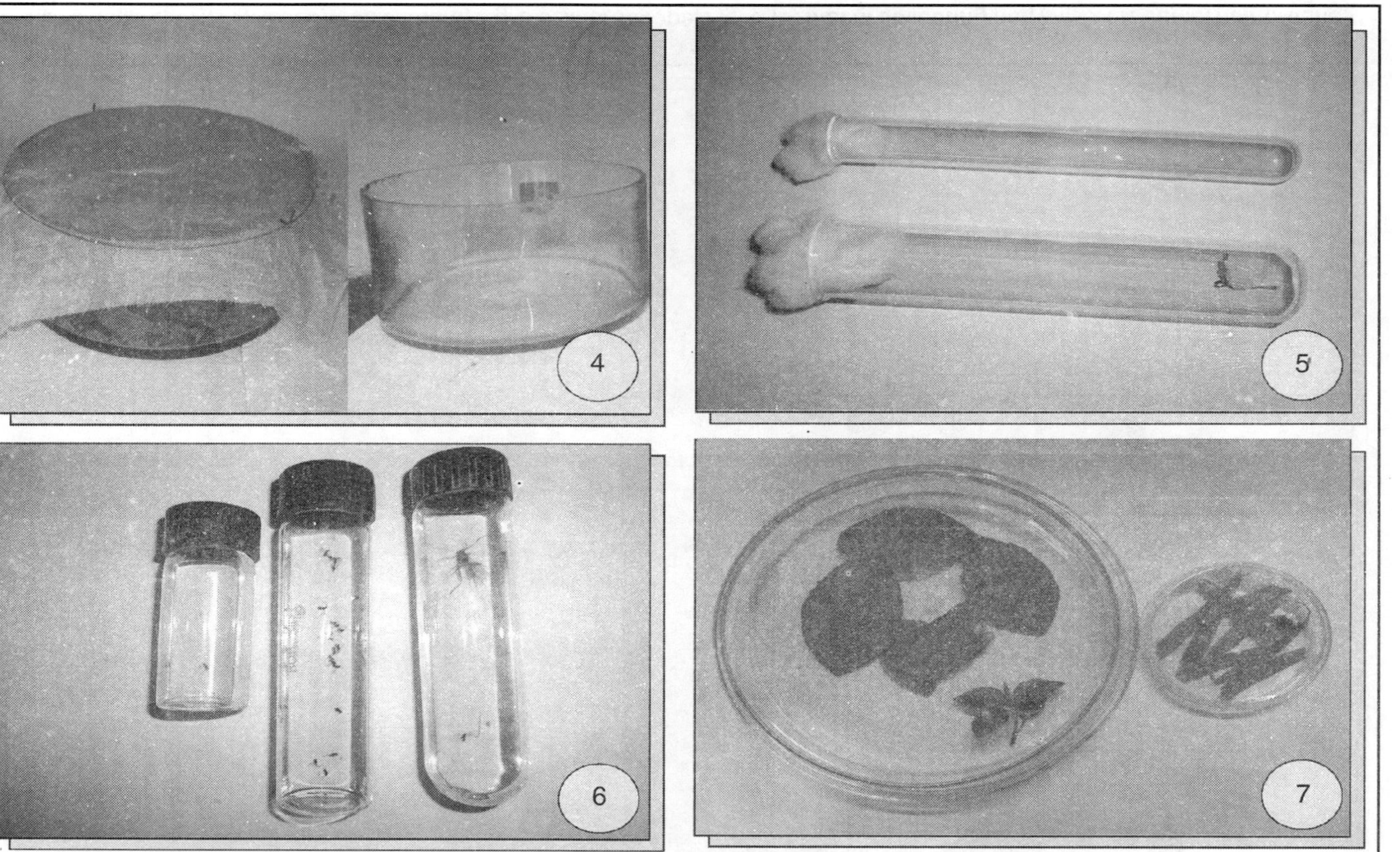

Plate - 2 (Figs. 4-7): Fig. 3.4: **Glass trough,** Fig. 3.5: **Test tubes,** Fig. 3.6: **Specimen tubes,** Fig 3.7: **Petri dishes**

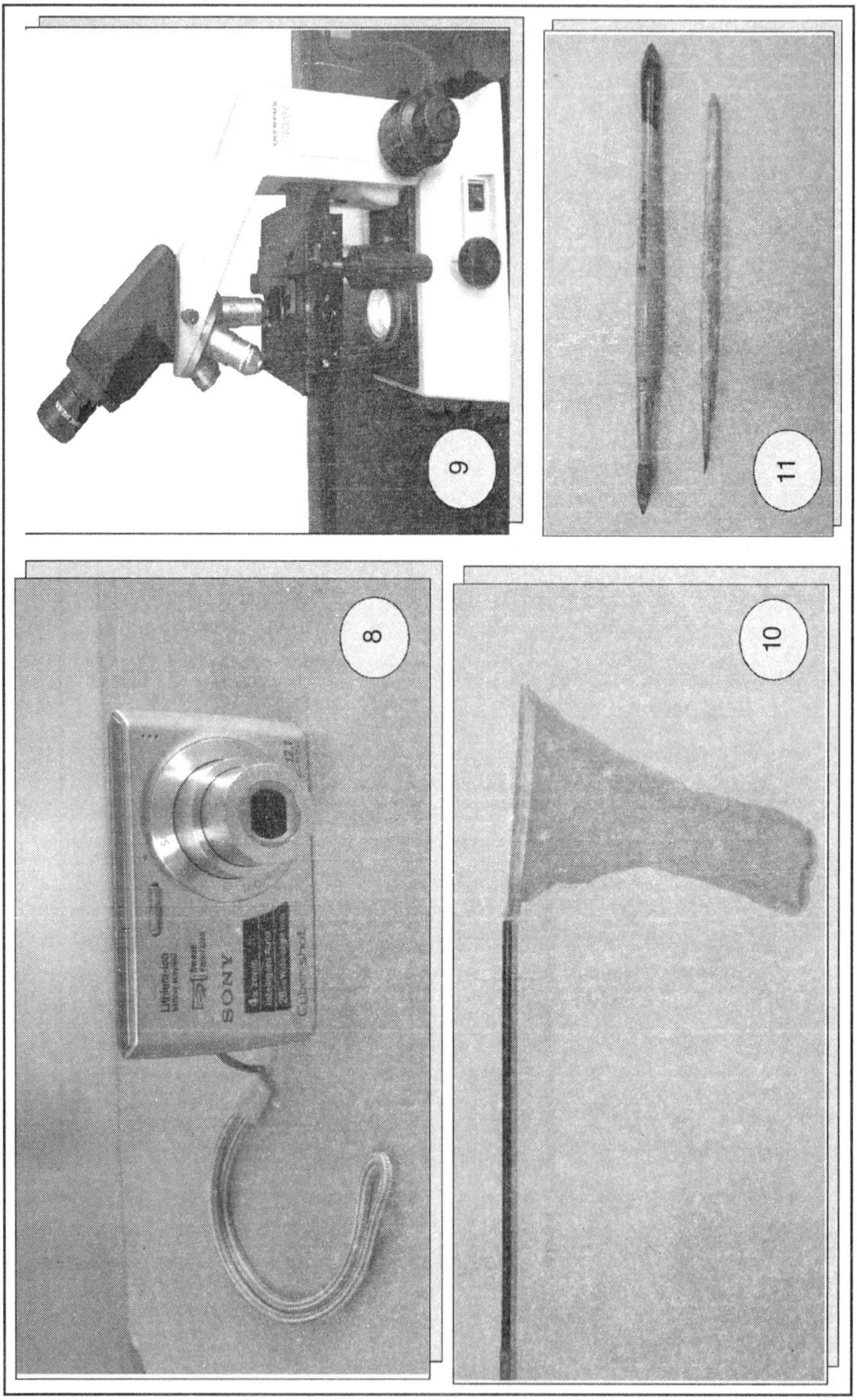

Plate - 3 (Figs. 8-11): Fig. 3.8: **Digital camera,** Fig. 3.9: **Microscope,** Fig. 3.10: **Insect collecting net,** Fig. 3.11: **Camel hair brushes**

Oven

Oven of size, 3.6×2.4 feet (height and width) has been used for drying adult parasitoids, moths and the permanent slides of parasitoids.

Chemicals

Following chemicals were used for preparation of slides and preserving the insects.

1. 10 per cent KOH.
2. 30 per cent, 50 per cent, 70 per cent and 100 per cent Ethyl alcohol grades.
3. Glacial acetic acid.
4. Xylene.
5. DPX/Canada Balsum.

REARING METHODS

1. Rearing of Pest Species

(a) Rearing of *A. moorei* (Plate 4, Figs. 3.12-3.17): The rearing of *A. moorei* was initiated by collecting the caterpillars from the sorghúm crops from study areas. The collected caterpillars were placed in rearing cages, fresh feed was given daily and cleaning was done periodically for maintaining sanitation in rearing cages. Caterpillars were caged together up to formation of pupae, thereafter pupae were placed separately in the plastic container. The newly emerged pair (♂ and ♀) of moth was caged in one container and allowed them to mate. After mating females were transferred to oviposition jar, which contained wrapped wet tissue paper or wet muslin cloth on which females laid their eggs. The eggs (Fig. 3.12) were collected with the help of camel hair brush and shifted into petri dishes with filter paper. After hatching from eggs the newly emerged caterpillars were transferred into the large size container (size 6.5×8cm) along with the leaves of sorghum (*Sorghum vulgare* Pers.) plants. Whereas, later instars (Figs. 3.13-3.15) were placed separately into small plastic containers (size 5×5cm) to avoid overcrowding. The larva of *A. moorei* was full grown in between 17-19 days and spins loose cocoon for pupation. The pupa (Fig. 3.16) was dark brown in colour and obtect type. During the rearing of *A. moorei*, the larvae were fed with leaves of *S. vulgare* and adult moths (Fig. 3.17) with 50 per cent honey solution.

(b) Rearing of *S. litura* (Plate 5, Figs. 3.18-3.23): The caterpillars of *S. litura* were collected from the field of soybean and were reared in plastic containers (size 6×8.5cm) to avoid the overcrowding up to pupation and adult emergence under laboratory conditions. The newly emerged pair (♂ and ♀) was kept separately in the plastic container,

Plate - 4 (Figs. 12-17): ***A. moorei:* Life cycle**. Fig. 3.12: **Eggs**, Fig 3.13: **First instar larvae,** Fig. 3.14: **Third instar larva,** Fig. 3.15: **Last instar larva,** Fig. 3.16: **Pupa,** Fig. 3.17: **Adult moth**

size 5×5cm. The container was wrapped internally with wet tissue paper on which female laid the eggs (Fig. 3.18). The eggs were collected with the help of camel hair brush and placed in the petri dishes which contained filter paper. The earlier instar caterpillars are gregarious (Fig. 3.19) hence kept in single glass trough and from third instar (Fig. 3.20) to last instar (Fig. 3.21) caterpillars were reared separately in containers up to pupation (Fig. 3.22) and finally adult moth (Fig. 3.23) formation. During the experiment caterpillars of *S. litura* early instars were fed with leaves of soybean and moths with 50 per cent honey solution.

(c) Rearing of *C. partellus* (Plate 6, Figs. 3.24-29): The caterpillars of *C. partellus* were collected from the fields of jowar and reared separately in plastic container up to pupation and adult emergence under the laboratory conditions (25±2°C temperature, 60±5 per cent Relative Humidity and 12 hr photoperiod). The newly emerged pair of moths was kept in separate plastic container (size 6×8.5cm) wrapped with wet tissue paper internally. In the plastic container jowar leaves were also placed for the egg laying purpose. The eggs (Fig. 3.24) were laid either on tissue paper or on the leaves, which were collected by camel hair brush and transferred in petri dishes with filter paper. The newly emerged caterpillars (Fig. 3.25) were transferred to plastic container for the further development. The later instars (Fig. 3.26-3.27) were reared separately up to development of pupae (Fig. 3.28) and adult (Fig. 3.29). During rearing of *C. partellus*, the caterpillars were fed with leaves and stem of jowar for early and later instars respectively whereas, moths with 50 per cent honey solution.

The above methods were adopted for obtaining sufficient number of hosts, for utilization in various experiments.

1. Rearing of Parasitoid Species

(a) Rearing of *A. bosei* (Braconidae) (Plate 7): The parasitized larvae of host *A. moorei* and cocoons of parasitoids were directly collected from the sorghum fields and culture was maintained in the laboratory. The newly emerged parasitoid pair (♂ and ♀) was shifted into the test tube for mating. The mated females were exposed to 50 early instar caterpillars in insect rearing cage at the rate of 5 females per cage. Parasitoid quickly oviposited their eggs into the host body therefore; more parasitized larvae were achieved within short period. The parasitized caterpillars were separated into petri dishes for further observations like: parasitoids or host emergence. During the experiment the larvae were fed with sorghum leaves while, the parasitoid adults with 50 per cent honey solution.

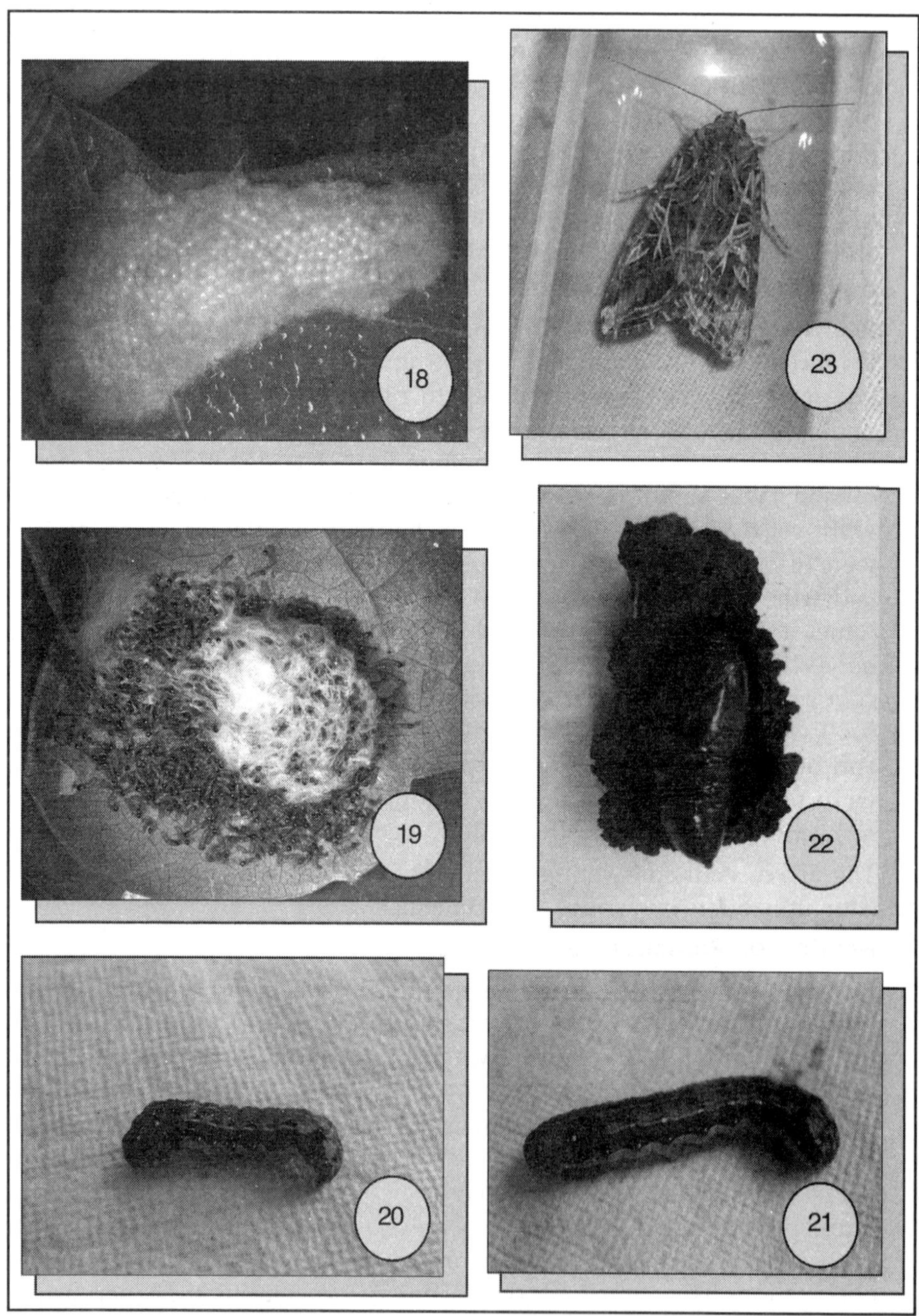

Plate - 5 (Figs. 18-23): ***S. litura:* Life Cycle**. Fig. 3.18: **Egg mass,** Fig. 3.19: **First instar larvae,** Fig. 3.20: **Third instar larva,** Fig. 3.21: **Last instar larva,** Fig. 3.22: **Pupa,** Fig. 3.23: **Adult moth**

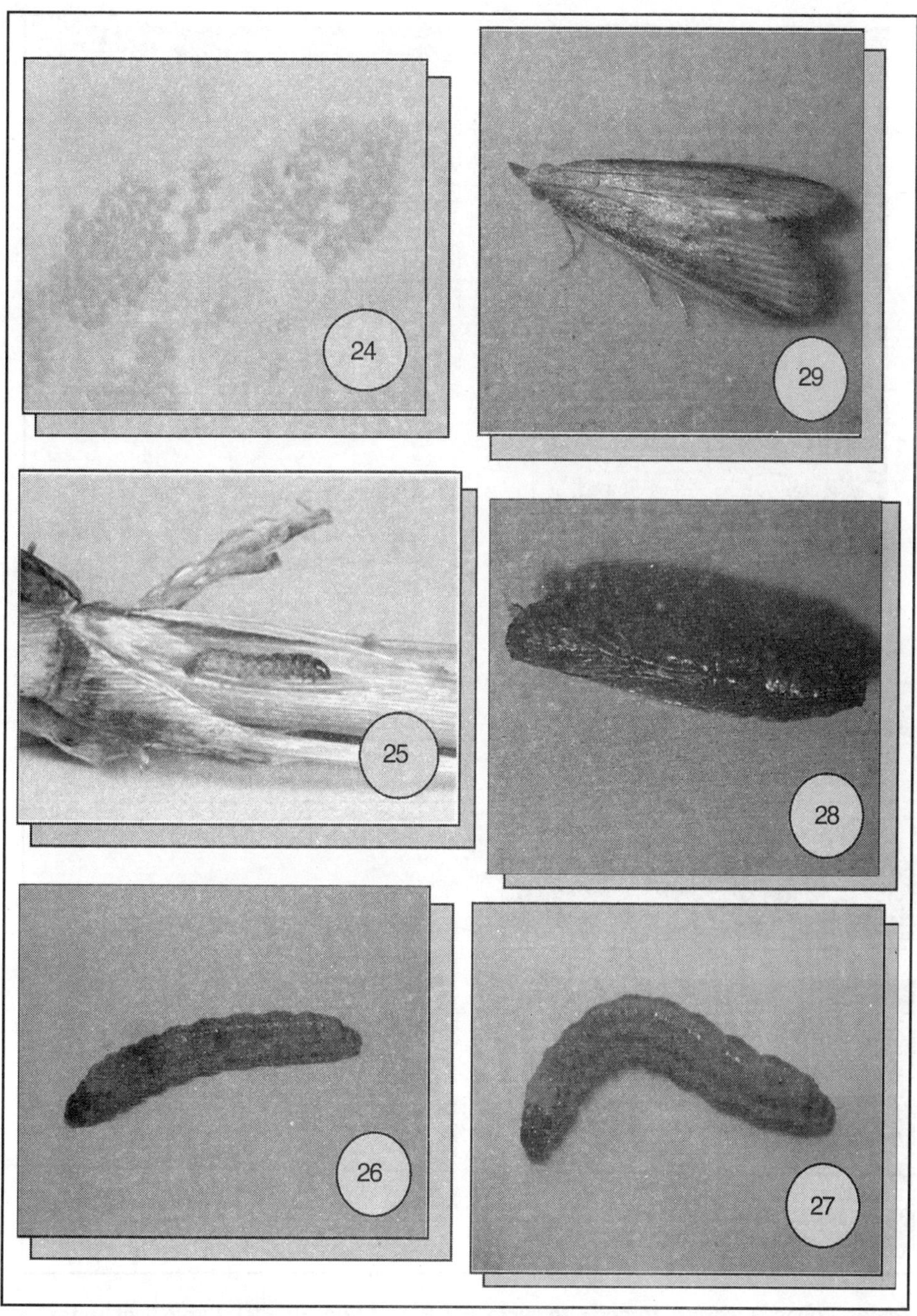

Plate - 6 (Figs. 24-29) ***C. partellus:* Life cycle.** Fig. 3.24: **Eggs,** Fig. 3.25: **Second instar larva,** Fig. 3.26: **Fourth instar larva,** Fig. 3.27: **Last instar larva,** Fig. 3.28: **Pupa,** Fig. 3.29: **Adult moth**

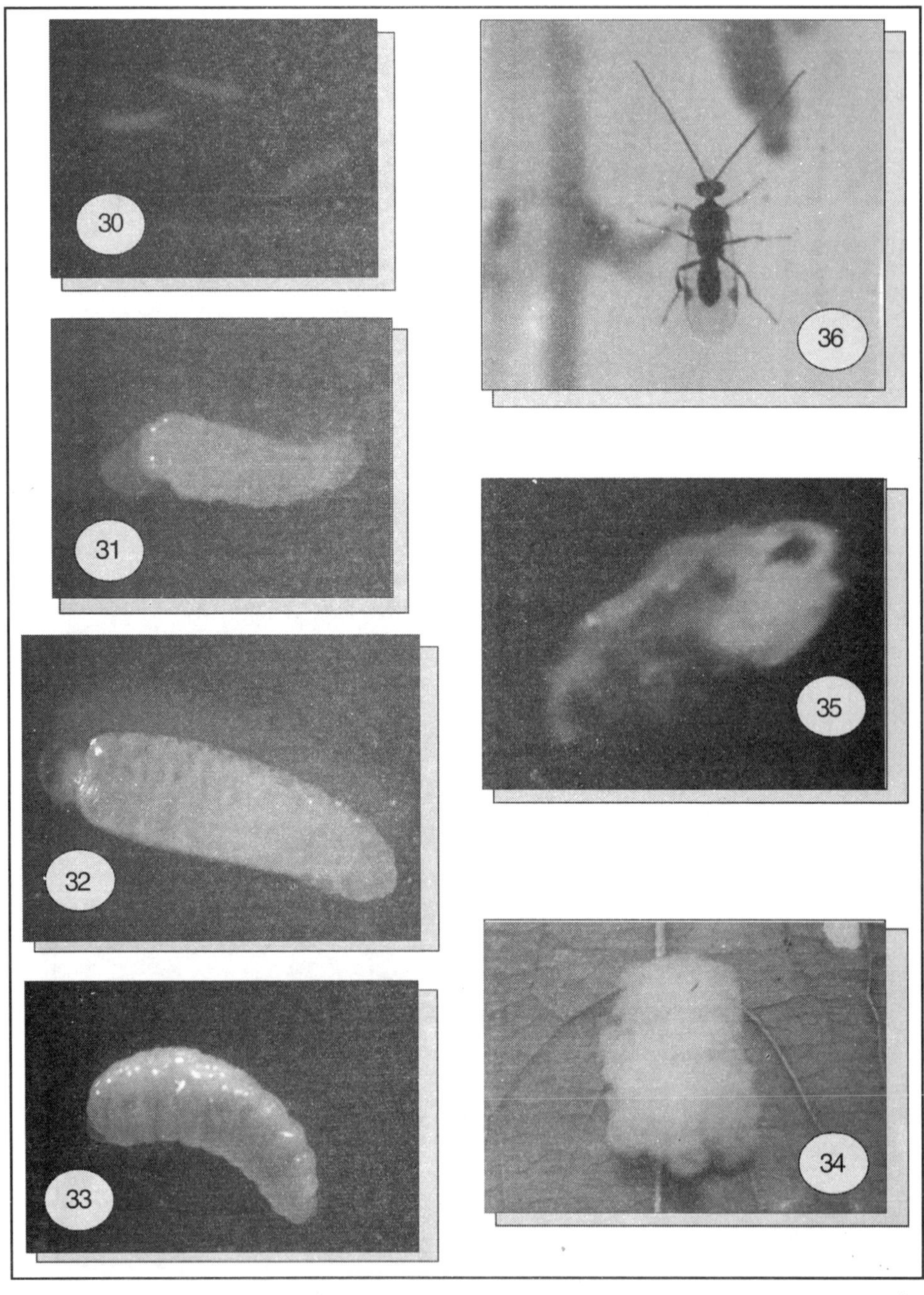

Plate - 7 (Figs. 30-36): ***A. bosei:* Life cycle.** Fig. 3.30: **Eggs,** Fig 3.31: **Larva first instar,** Fig. 3.32: **Larva second instar,** Fig. 3.33: **Larva third instar,** Fig. 3.34: **Cocoons,** Fig. 3.35: **Pupa,** Fig. 3.36: **Adult female**

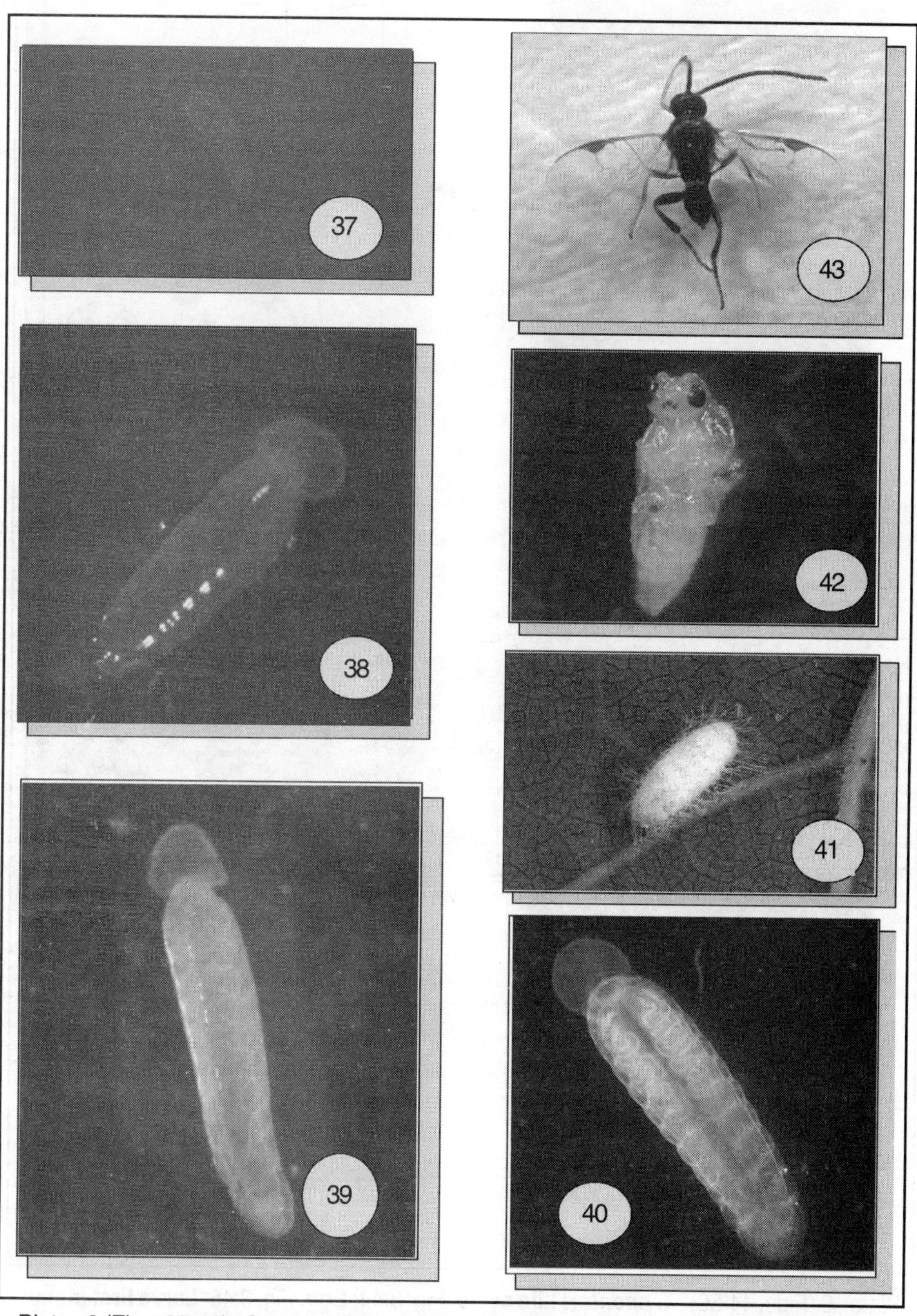

Plate - 8 (Figs. 37-43): ***G. spodopterae:* Life cycle.** Fig. 3.37: **Egg,** Fig. 3.38: **Larva first instar,** Fig. 3.39: **Larva second instar,** Fig. 3.40: **Larva third instar,** Fig. 3.41: **Cocoon,** Fig. 3.42: **Pupa,** Fig. 3.43: **Adult female**

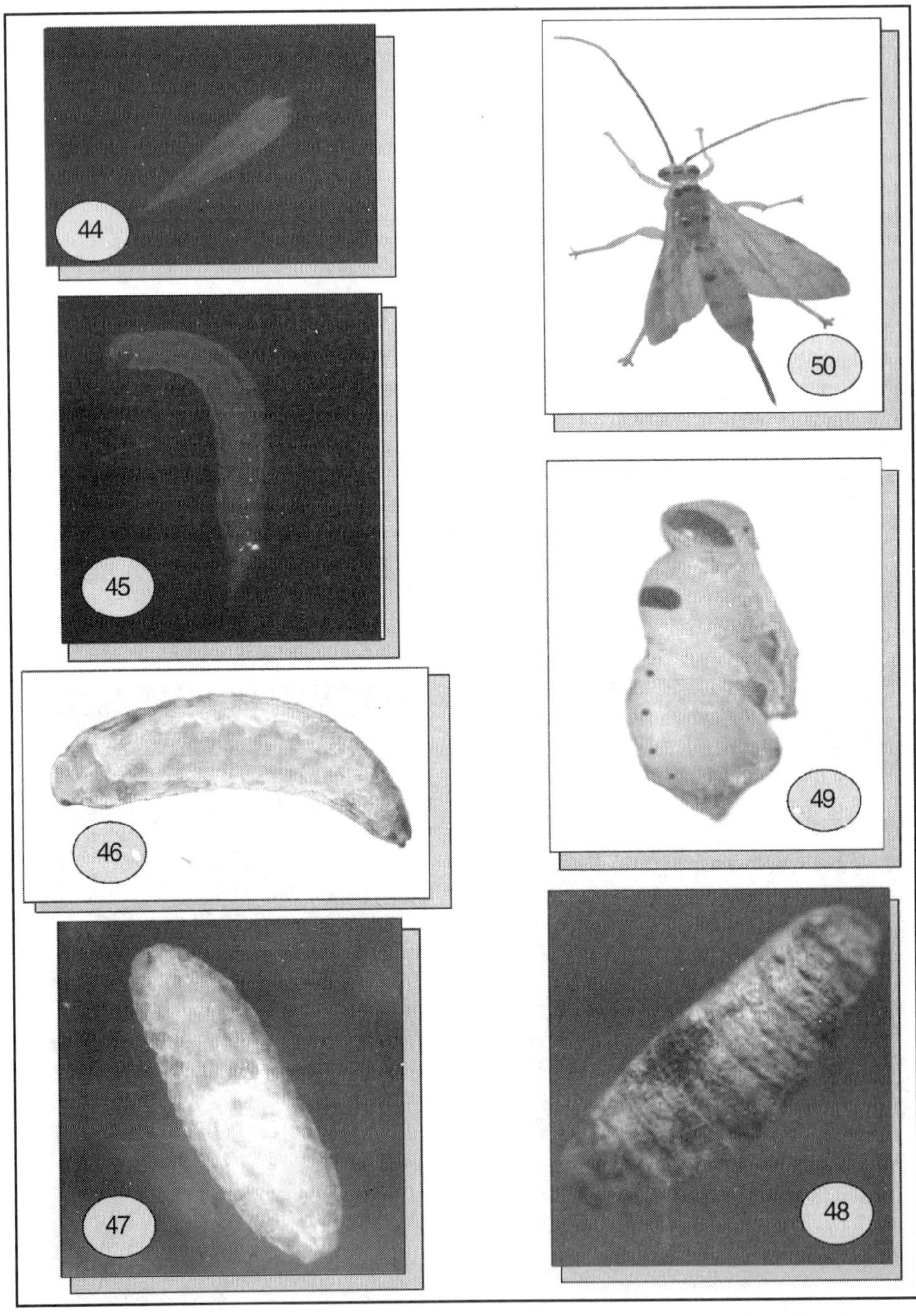

Plate - 9 (Figs. 44-50): ***X. pedator:* Life cycle.** Fig. 3.44: **Egg,** Fig. 3.45: **Larva first instar,** Fig. 3.46: **Larva third instar,** Fig. 3.47: **Larva fourth instar,** Fig. 3.48: **Cocoon,** Fig. 3.49: **Pupa,** Fig. 3.50: **Adult female**

(*b*) Rearing of *G. spodopterae* (Braconidae) (Plate 8): The primary culture of parasitoids was brought from the field through cocoon collection and they were placed individually in test tubes. After adult emerged from cocoons, the pair (♂ and ♀) was caged in the single test tube for mating. The mated females were separated in petri dishes along with the second instar caterpillars of *S. litura* for one hour period. After oviposition, the caterpillars were reared individually in small plastic containers by providing leaves of soybean up to formation of parasitoid cocoon or pupa of *S. litura*. The parasitized caterpillar developed in to cocoons of parasitoid by escaping out from the body of host caterpillars and killing the pest.

(*c*) Rearing of *X. pedator* (Ichneumonidae) (Plate 9): The cocoons and adults of *X. pedator* were collected directly from the field of jowar. Cocoons were reared separately to avoid the mixing of sexes. Newly emerged pair of parasitoid (♂ and ♂) was caged in one test tube to study their mating behaviour. Mating was observed immediately after caging. Five mated females of *X. pedator* were exposed to pupae of *C. partellus* in one insect cage. Parasitoid rapidly deposited their egg into host body and thus, more parasitized hosts were obtained within short period. After parasitization the host pupae were kept individually in plastic containers for further development. During the experiment, parasitoids were fed with 50 per cent honey solution.

The above methods were adopted for getting sufficient number of parasitoids and further used for various experiments adopted in the present work.

Biology of Parasitoids

LIFECYCLE OF PARASITOIDS

INTRODUCTION

Parasitoids show complex and interesting biology. The biological aspects are useful in mass rearing technique of parasitoids. They often check the pest population in many of pest insects hence they have tremendous economic importance (Doutt, 1959; De Batch Poul, 1964; Fincke *et al*. 1990; Beyarslan and Aydogdu, 2013).

Parasitoids are widely reported from insect orders like: Hymenoptera, Diptera, Strepsiptera, Hemiptera, Lepidoptera, etc. Out of which Hymenoptera ranks first, having several families which are parasitic in nature. The families Braconidae and Ichneumonidae rank first and second respectively, each includes more than one lakh species from the world. The family Tachinidae of order Diptera allotted third position promisingly with more than one thousand five hundred species world wide.

There is a difference between the parasitoids and true parasites, as parasitoids are entomophagus insects, they do not show heterocism and whose larvae are parasitic while adults are free living. Their hosts are only insects and they possess comparatively larger size than that of true parasites.

Study of immature forms of parasitoids can enhance the reliable understanding of the species. For better recognization of parasitoids, their proper lifecycle and duration of immature stages is essential part. The lifecycle data is also helpful for identification of species.

The present topic is devoted for lifecycle studies of *A. bosei* (Braconidae), a parasitoid of red hairy caterpillar *A. moorei, G. spodopterae* (Braconidae), a parasitoid of Tobacco caterpillar *S. litura* and *X. pedator* (Ichneumonidae), a parasitoid of lepidopteran stem borer *C. partellus.*

Materials and Methods

Rearing of parasitoids and their hosts was initiated under the laboratory conditions 25±2°C temperature, 60±5 per cent Relative Humidity (R.H.) and 12 hr photoperiod. This culture was further used to study the lifecycle of parasitoids. The lifecycle of all parasitoids were studied by exposing proper hosts with optimum age towards the parasitoid. The hosts were exposed to parasitoids for 24 hr and adequate numbers of parasitized hosts were obtained. The immature stages of parasitoids were collected by dissecting the parasitized hosts. The lifecycle of parasitoids were studied by maintaining the records of egg laying, incubation, larval as well as pupal period and adult longevity. For confirming the results the whole experiments were replicated for 5 times.

Results

1. Life Cycle of *A. bosei* (Plate 1, Figs. 4.1 to 4.7)

The braconid parasitoid parasitizes the larvae of *A. moorei*. The duration of life stages of *A. bosei* is shown in Table 4.1. The total developmental period ranges from 13-18 days.

Eggs (Fig. 4.1)

The female deposited eggs in the body of host larva. As they are gregarious, on an average 20-30 eggs were laid by the single female in one host species. The eggs were white, thin walled and typically hymenopteriform. After oviposition the size of eggs were increased rapidly. The average egg hatching period was 2.90 (±0.54) days.

Larva (Fig. 4.2-4.4)

A. bosei showed 3 larval instars. The first instar was with broad head, translucent body. The first two instars were vasiculated and later one was hymenopteriform. Three days after hatching head of larva became narrow and the body was more opaque. The vesicle of first and second instar was about rounded in shape and milky white colour. The first instar lasted for 4 days.

The larva of second instar possessed a narrow head. The body was straight, white and cylindrical. The swollen part of head looks quite flat with slight elevation. Tracheal system shows single lateral longitudinal trunk (Fig. 4.3b). The second instar lasts for about 3 days.

The third instar larvae were opaque white. The body segments were clearly visible. Tracheal system showed two longitudinal trunks and one transverse commissure with 8 pairs of spiracles (Fig. 4.4b). The body of larva tapered slightly towards both ends. The mouth parts were well developed. The body was well segmented and larger in size than earlier instars. The mature larvae emerged from the host by rupturing the host body and spinning cottony white cocoons. The third instar stage lasted for 2 days. The average larval period was 8.93 (±0.82) days.

Cocoons (Fig. 4.5)

The last instar larvae escaped out from the host body and formed cottony white densely spun, cylindrical cocoons which were rounded at both ends. *A. bosei* was gregarious parasitoid. Hence, prepared cocoon colony.

Pupa (Fig. 4.6)

The pupa was grayish initially except for eyes which were dark brown in colour. Later, became darker and darker and finally brownish black. The average pupal stage lasted for 4.03 (±0.52) days.

Adult (Fig. 4.7)

Adults were black with head, thorax and abdomen. Female showed long characterised antennae and very fine ovipositor. The average development period from egg deposition to adult emergence lasted for 15.87 (±1.23) days.

2. Life Cycle of *G. spodopterae* (Plate 2, Figs. 4.8 to 4.14)

The braconid parasitoid parasitized the larvae of *S. litura*. The duration of life stages of *G. spodopterae* are shown in Table 4.2. The total developmental period ranged from 19.5-22.5 days whereas adult longevity varied on different food stuff ranging from 9-14 days.

Egg (Fig. 4.8)

The female deposited egg in the body of host larva. As they were solitary parasitoid, single egg was laid by the female in one host species. The eggs were gray, thin walled and typically showed hymenopteriform. After oviposition the size of eggs were increased rapidly. The average egg hatching period was 3.30 (±0.41) days.

Larva (Fig. 4.9-4.11)

G. spodopterae showed 3 larval instars. First instar (Fig. 4.9) was with translucent body and broad head. The first two instars were vesiculated and third instar was hymenopteriform. The head of larva became narrower afterwards and the body was more opaque. The larvae were with swollen and rounded head and transparent body with vesicle at posterior end. The first instar stage lasted for about 5 days.

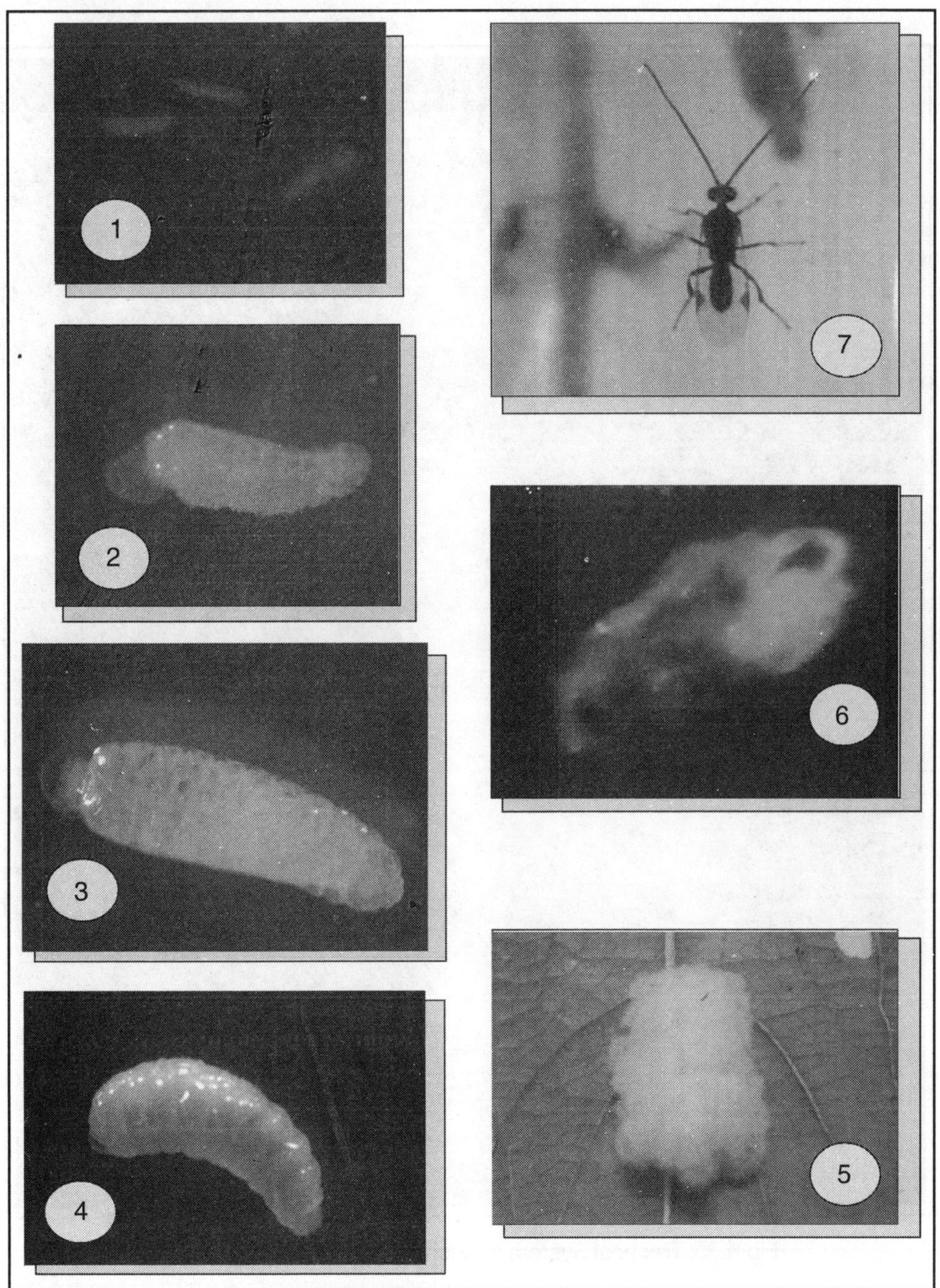

Plate - 1 (Figs. 1-7): **Life cycle of *A. bosei:*** Fig. 4.1: **Eggs,** Fig 4.2: **Larva first instar,** Fig. 4.3: **Larva second instar,** Fig. 4.4: **Larva third instar,** Fig. 4.5: **Cocoons,** Fig. 4.6: **Pupa,** Fig. 4.7: **Adult female**

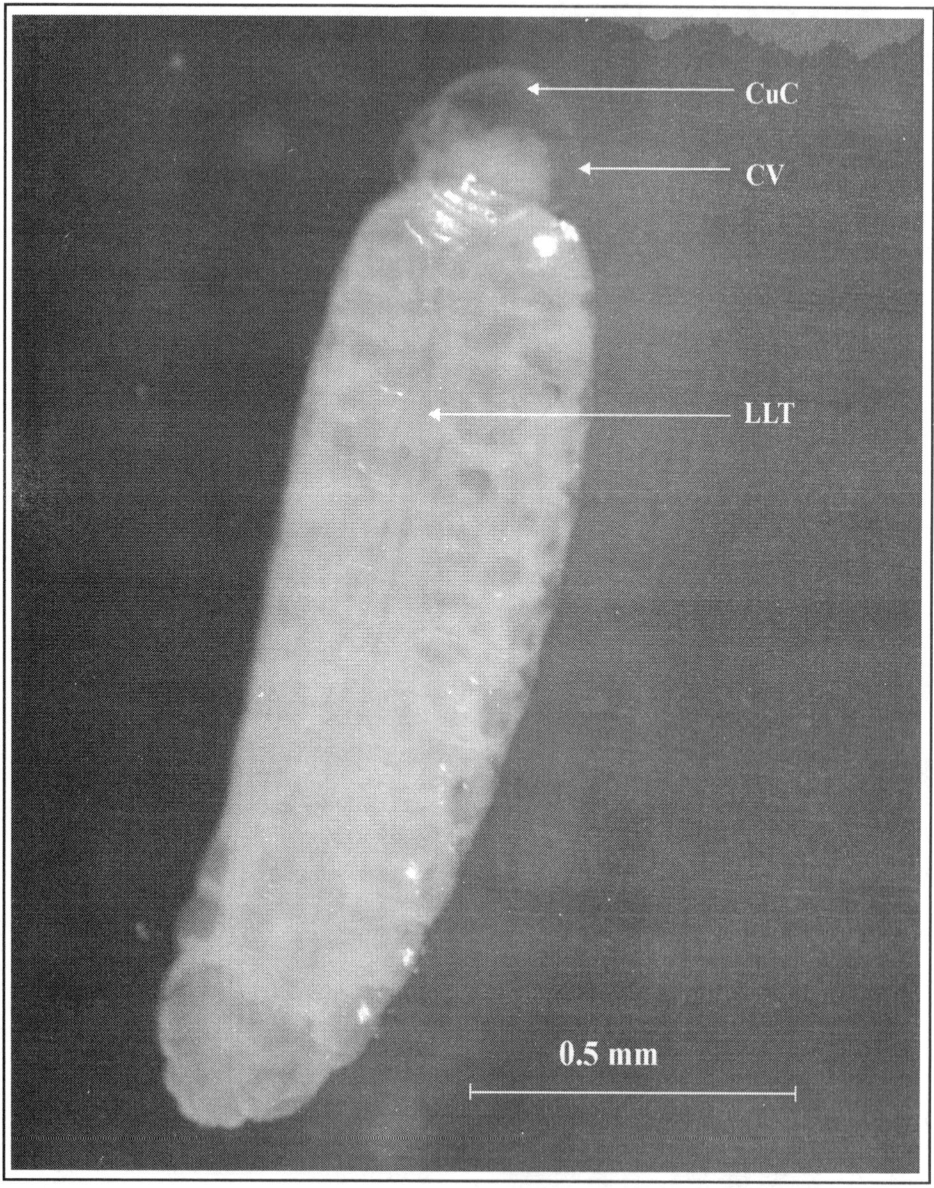

Fig. 4.3b: **Tracheal System of Second Instar larva of *A. bosei***

CV - Caudal vesicle

CuC - Columnar cells

LTT - Lateral longitudinal trunk

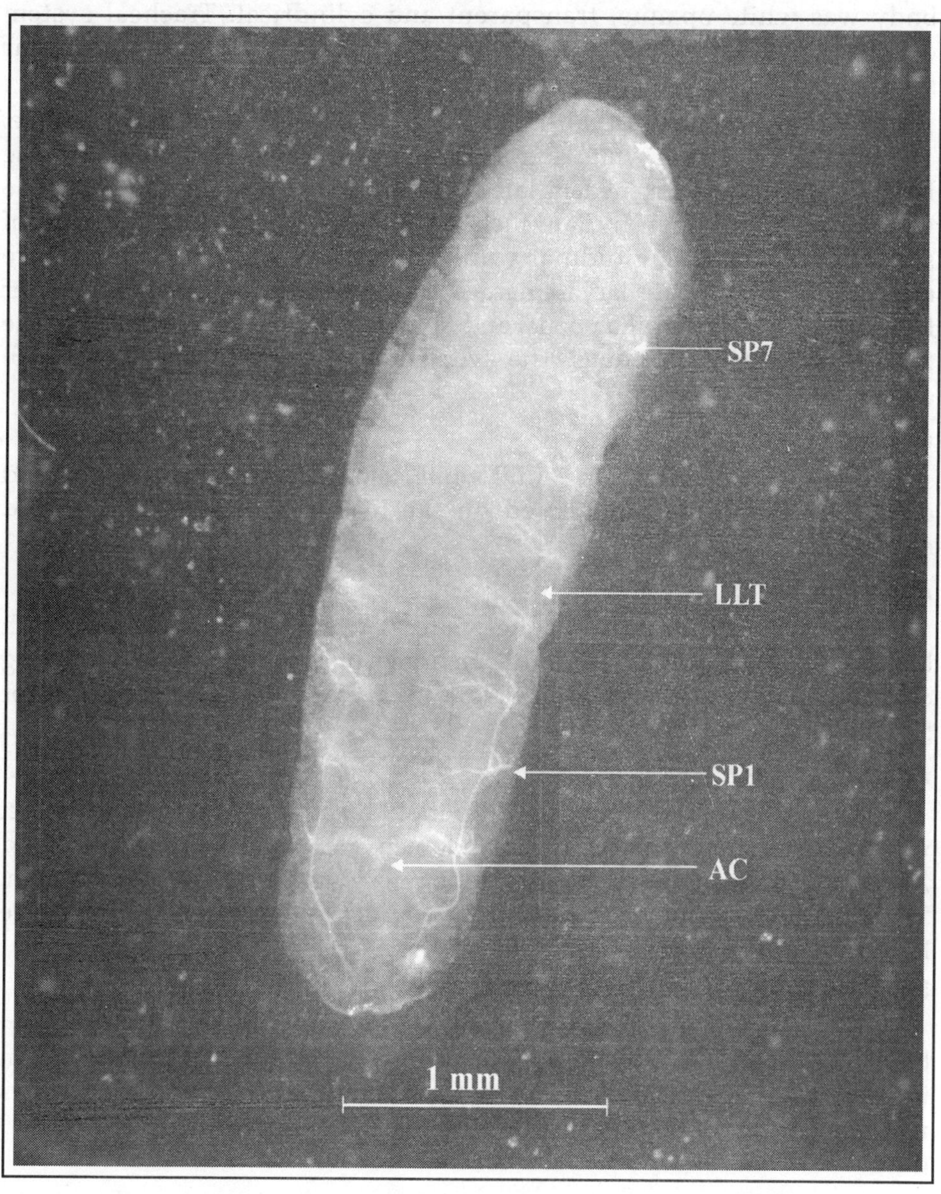

Fig. 4.4b: **Tracheal System of Third Instar larva of *A. bosei***

AC - Anterior Commissure

SP1 - First Spiracle

SP7 - Seventh Spiracle

LTT - Lateral longitudinal trunk

The second instar (Fig. 4.10) was with well-defined 13 segments. The body was white opaque, transparent and cylindrical. Tracheal system exhibits single lateral longitudinal trunks (Fig. 4.10b). The second instar stage lasted for about 4 days. This stage was vesiculated.

The body segments of third instar (Fig. 4.11) larvae were clearly visible. The body was opaque white and slightly tapered towards both ends. The larval length was shortened in late stage and was hymenopteriform. The vesicle was withdrawn by late instar. Tracheal system shows 8 pairs of spiracles and two longitudinal trunks and one transverse commissure (Fig. 4.11b). The mature larva emerged from the host by killing them later feed on the host caterpillar body and spinning cottony white cocoon. The third instar lasted for 3 days. The average larval period was 12.60 (±0.76) days.

Cocoon (Fig. 4.12)

Cocoon was small in size, dull white coloured with glossy nature and cylindrical shape and observed on the leaves of plants in the field conditions.

Pupa (Fig. 4.13)

The pupa at first was opaque white. Later, it became dark brownish black when full grown. The adult emerged out from cocoon by making circular opening at the anterior side. The average pupal stage lasted for 5.07 (±0.67) days.

Adult (Fig. 4.14)

Adults were dark brown with petiolate abdomen and with distinct wings extending beyond the tip of abdomen. Head and thorax were black. Abdomen, antennae, hind legs, femora, and ovipositor were dark brown. The average development period from egg deposition to adult emergence lasted for 20.97 (±0.95) days.

3. Life Cycle of *X. pedator* (Plate 3, Figs. 4.15 to 4.21)

The ichneumon parasitoid parasitized the pupae of lepidopteran stem borer like: *C. partellus*. The durations of life stages of *X. pedator* are shown in Table 4.3. The average development period ranged from 27.50-32.50 days whereas adult longevity varied on different food stuff ranging from 12-19 days.

Egg (Fig. 4.15)

X. pedator is a solitary parasitoid, single egg was laid by the female in one host species. The female deposited egg in the body of host. The eggs were yellowish white, oval, thin walled, tapering at one end and slightly curved typically showed hymenopteriform. After oviposition the size of eggs increased rapidly. The average egg hatching period was 4.33 (±0.67) days after ovipositing in the host body.

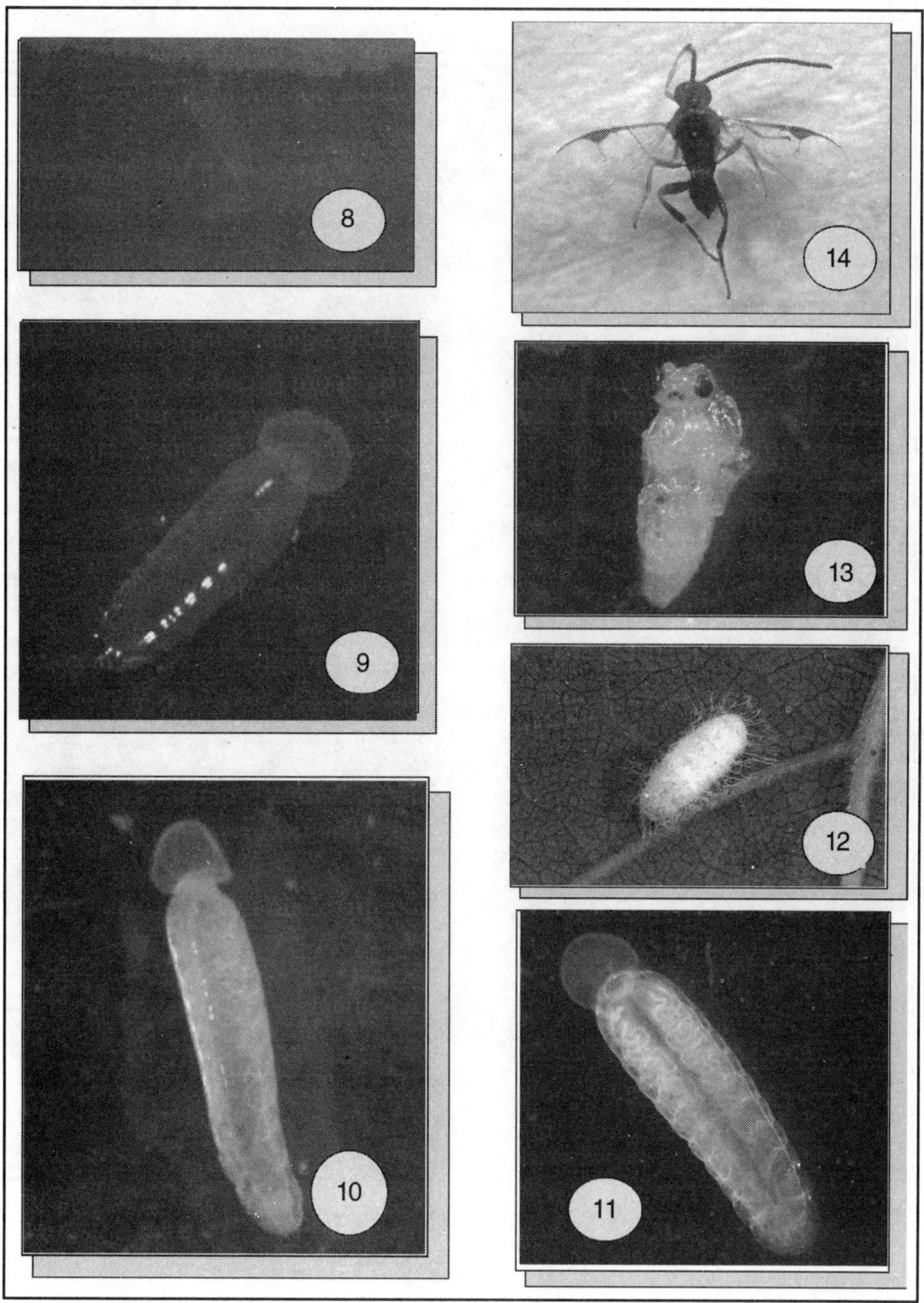

Plate - 2 (Figs. 8-14): **Life Cycle of *G. spodopterae:*** Fig. 4.8: **Egg,** Fig. 4.9: **Larva first instar,** Fig. 4.10: **Larva second instar,** Fig. 4.11: **Larva third instar,** Fig. 4.12: **Cocoon,** Fig. 4.13: **Pupa,** Fig. 4.14: **Adult female**

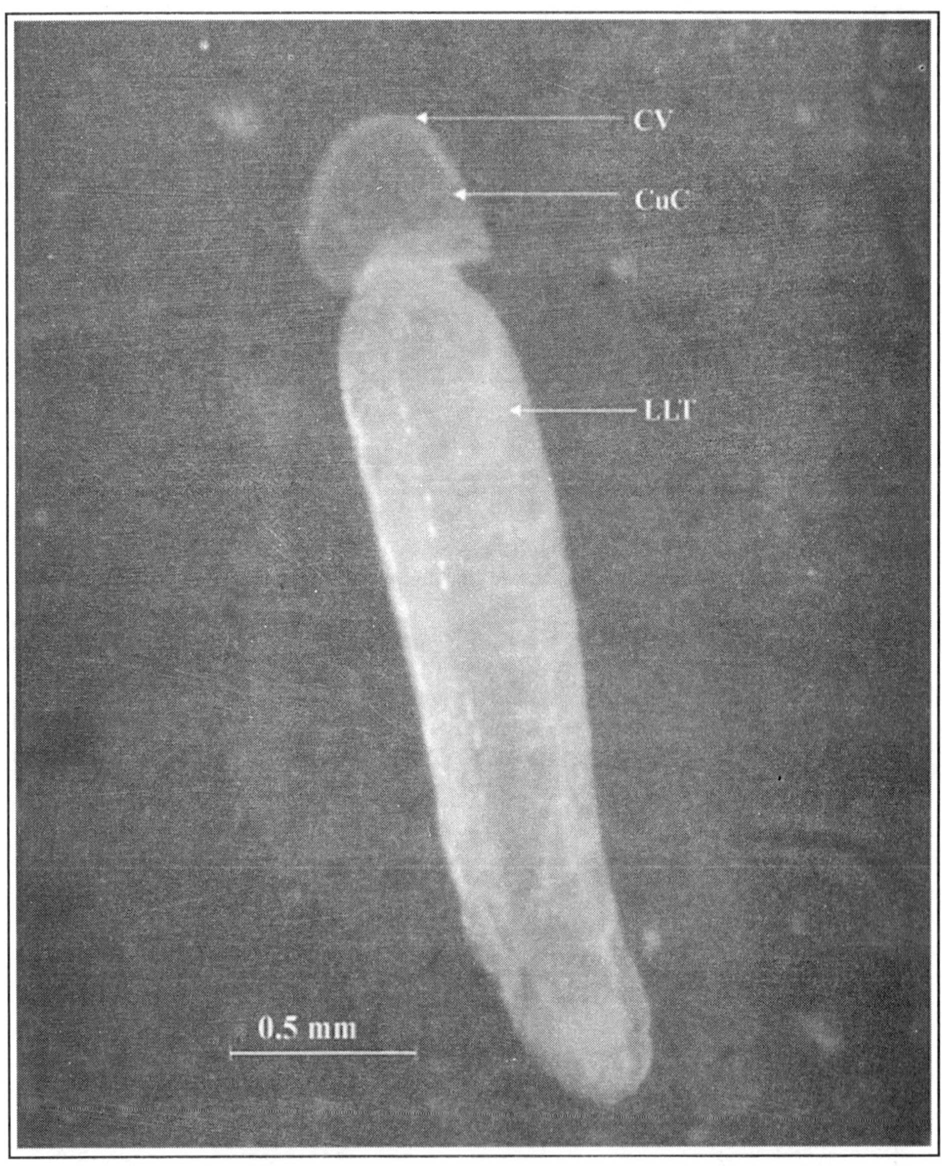

Fig. 4.10b: **Tracheal System of Second Instar larva of *G. spodoptera***

CV - Caudal vesicle

CuC - Columnar Cells

LTT - Lateral longitudinal trunk

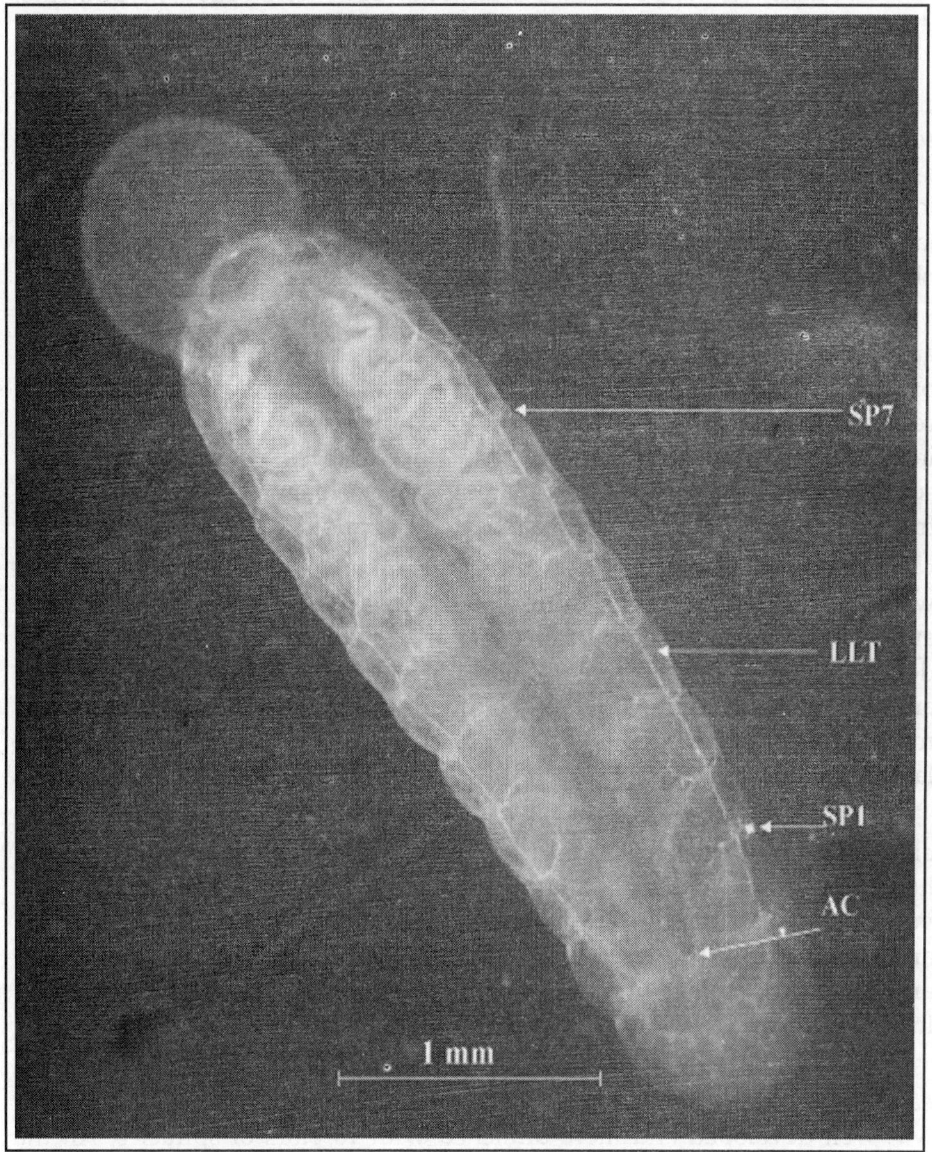

Fig. 4.11b: **Tracheal System of Third Instar larva of *G. spodopterae***

AC - Anterior Commissure

SP1 - First Spiracle

SP7 - Seventh Spiracle

LTT - Lateral longitudinal trunk

Larva (Fig. 4.16-4.18)

X. pedator showed 5 larval instars. First three were caudate type while, the later two instars were hymenopteriform.

The first instar (Fig. 4.16) larva was translucent with light yellow coloured body. The larva bears characteristic long tapering tail. All 13 segments were distinct and no variation was noticed between the thoracic as well as abdominal segments. Tracheal system showed a single longitudinal trunk (Fig. 4.16b). The first instar stage lasted for 3 days. The tapering tail was approximately half of the body length. Spiracles were not observed on the first instar of *X. pedator*.

The larva of second instar was opaque creamy white to yellow with apparently uneven body shape with short tail. The complete disappearance of tail was observed afterwards. The head and tail were considerably reduced in second instar while, the body increased in size. The second instar was different from first by their increased size, reduced tail, more sclerotized head and further branching of two longitudinal trunks of the tracheal system. The second instar lasted for about 2 days.

The third instar (Fig. 4.17) was also opaque yellow. The body segments were clearly observed. The third instar differs from second by larger size and also complete disappearance of tail. The tracheal system was well developed but spiracles were not observed yet (Fig. 4.17b). Both the caudal and cephalic ends were similarly rounded at the both ends. The head was more sclerotized, swollen and dark brown in colour. The third instar stage lasted for 2 days.

The fourth instar (Fig. 4.18) was of hymenopteriform with very soft, elongated and yellow coloured body with well-developed and sclerotized head and mouth parts. The larva increased rapidly in size and became voracious feeder. It showed elongated body shape with tapering cephalic and caudal ends. The larva was with well-developed 10 pairs of spiracles and tracheal system with two lateral longitudinal trunks having lateral loop (Fig. 4.18b). This stage lasted for 3 days.

The fifth instar was also hymenopteriform. The larva was opaque white earlier and became shiny yellow at the time of maturity. The tracheal system was well developed and more branched with 10 pairs of spiracles. All the body segments were distinct, head was strongly sclerotized and larval length shortened. At this stage larva came out of the host body and constructed cocoon. This is solitary parasitoid hence single cocoon was constructed. This stage lasted for 3 days. The average total larval period was 20.10 (±1.24) days.

Cocoon (Fig. 4.19)

Cocoons were brown coloured with irregular black spots and glossy with barrel shape. Peduncle was not observed with cocoon. The parasitoid showed solitary nature.

Pupa (Fig. 4.20)

The pupa was creamy white to light yellow, initially, later became dark except for eyes and some part of thorax which were black in colour with black markings on the abdomen, finally pupa became brownish dark. The adult emerged out through cocoon by making opening at the cephalic end. The average pupal stage lasted for 5.97 (±0.44) days.

Adult (Fig. 4.21)

Adults were shiny yellow with black eyes and very attractive black marking on head, thorax and abdomen. Female possessed long ovipositor. The average development period from egg deposition to adult emergence lasted for 30.40 (±1.33) days.

Table 4.1: Developmental period of *A. bosei*

Sr. No.	Egg Period (Days)	Larval Period (Days)	Pupal Period (Days)	Total Period from Egg Deposition to Adult Emergence	Sex
1.	3.00	9.00	3.50	15.50	♂
2.	2.50	7.00	4.00	13.50	♂
3.	3.00	7.50	4.00	14.50	♀
4.	2.50	9.00	3.50	15.00	♂
5.	2.50	8.50	4.00	15.00	♀
6.	2.50	10.00	4.50	17.00	♀
7.	3.50	9.00	4.00	16.50	♂
8.	3.00	9.50	3.50	16.00	♀
9.	2.50	9.00	3.50	15.00	♀
10.	4.00	9.50	4.50	18.00	♂
11.	3.50	10.00	4.00	17.50	♀
12.	3.00	9.00	4.00	16.00	♂
13.	2.00	9.00	4.00	15.00	♂
14.	2.50	8.50	5.50	16.50	♀
15.	3.50	9.50	4.00	17.00	♀
Average	2.90	8.93	4.03	15.87	
SE	±0.54	±0.82	±0.52	±1.23	

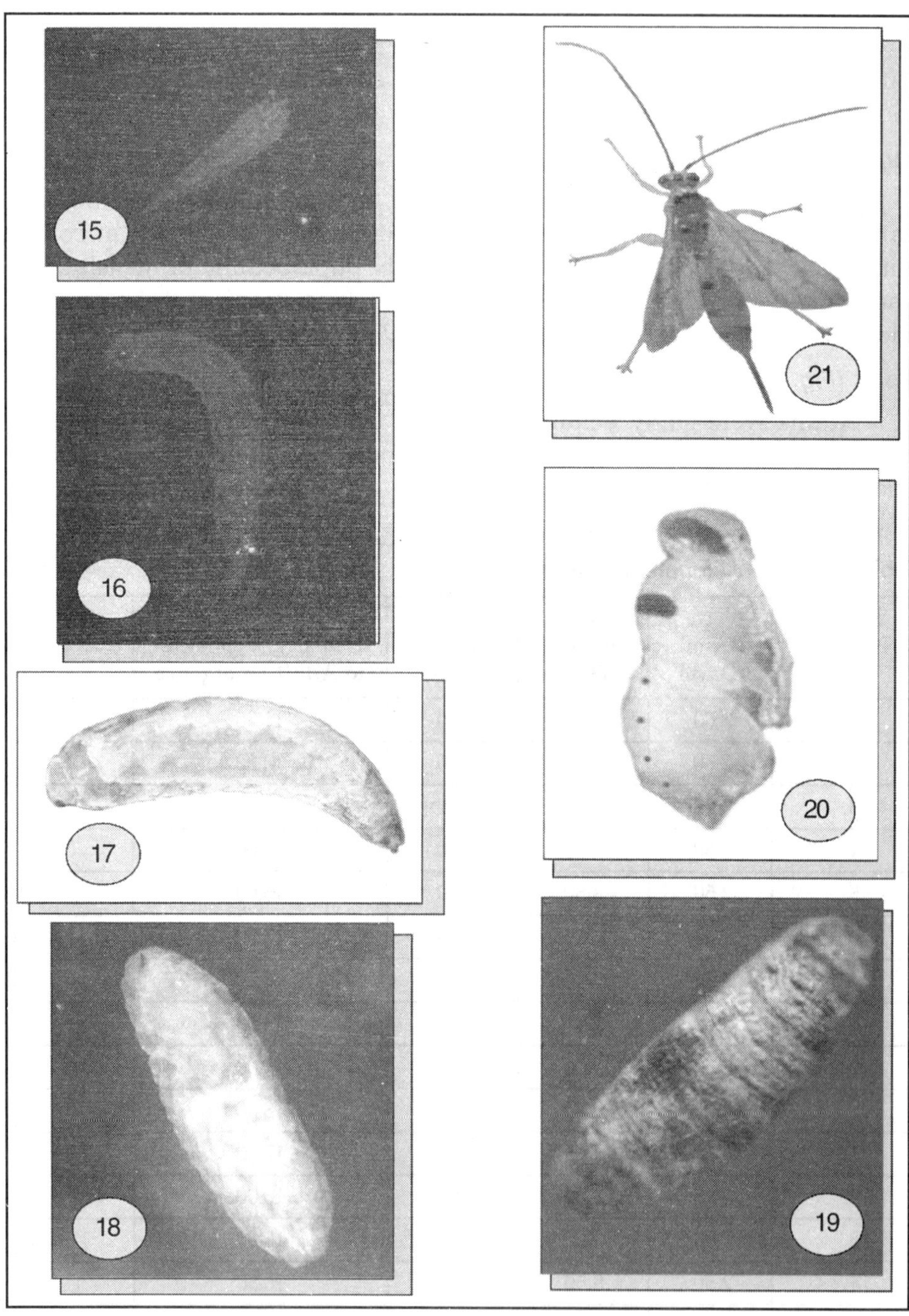

Plate - 3 (Figs. 15-21): **Life cycle of *X. pedator:*** Fig. 4.15: **Egg,** Fig. 4.16: **Larva first instar,** Fig. 4.17: **Larva third instar,** Fig. 4.18: **Larva fourth instar,** Fig. 4.19: **Cocoon,** Fig. 4.20: **Pupa,** Fig. 4.21: **Adult female**

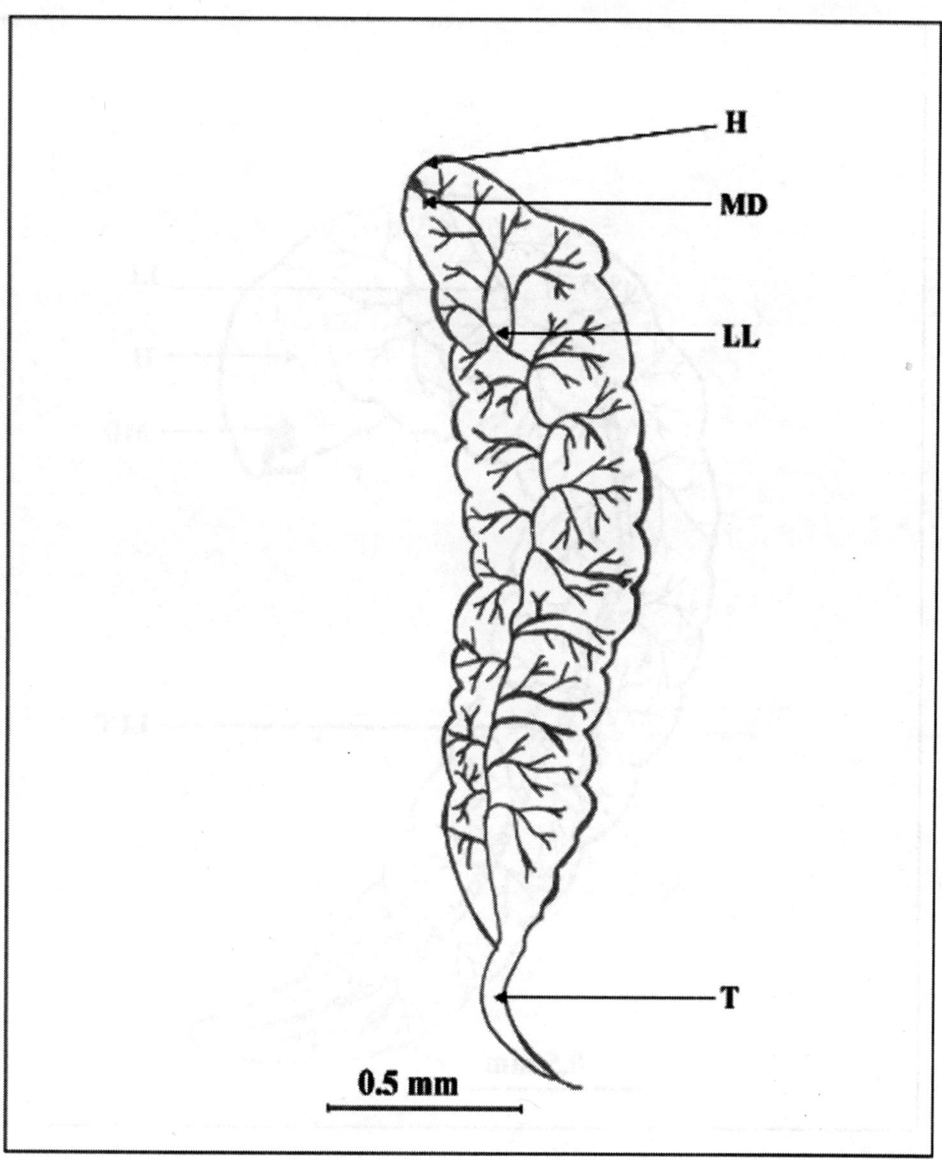

Fig. 4.16b: **Tracheal System of First Instar larva of *X. pedator***

H - Head

MD - Mandible

LL - Loop

T - Tail

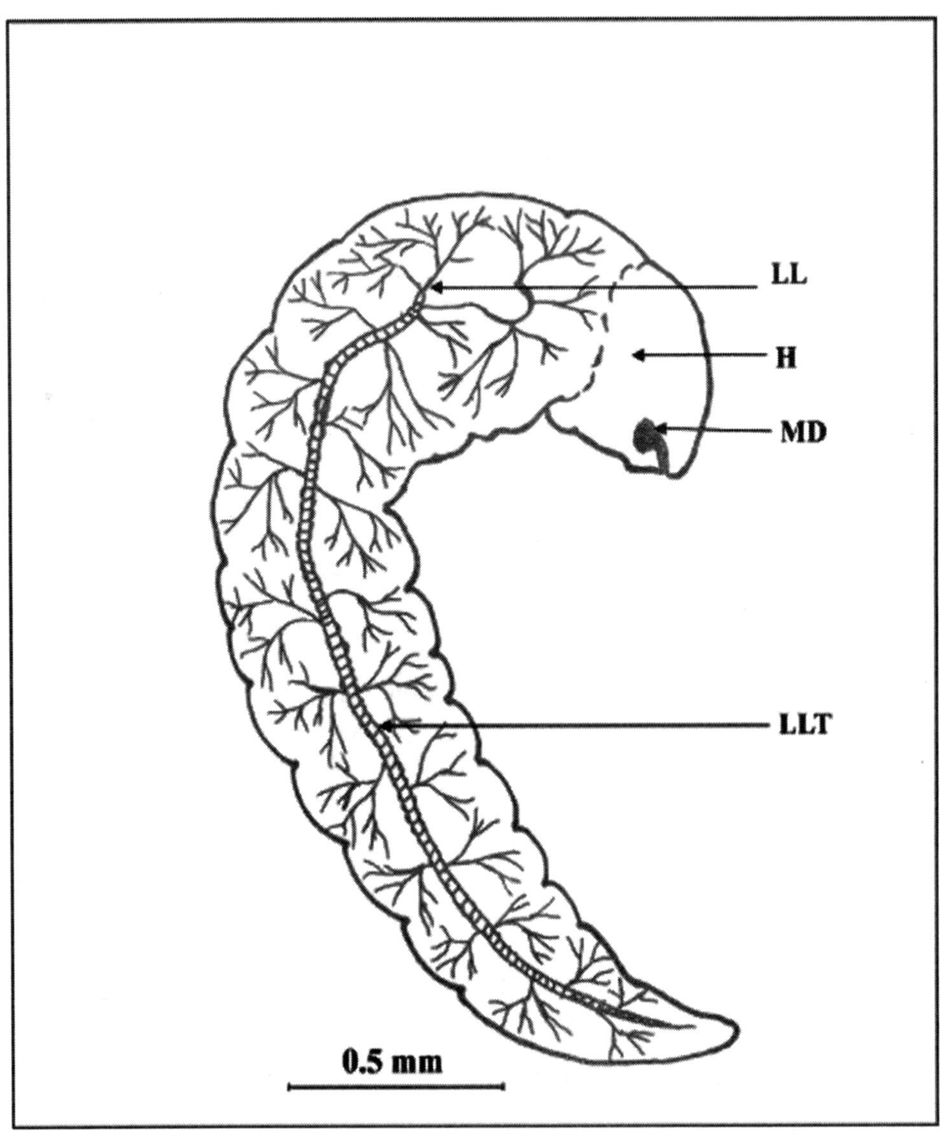

Fig. 4.17b: **Tracheal System of Third Instar larva of *X. pedator***

H - Head

MD - Mandible

LL - Loop

LLT - Lateral Longitudinal Trunk

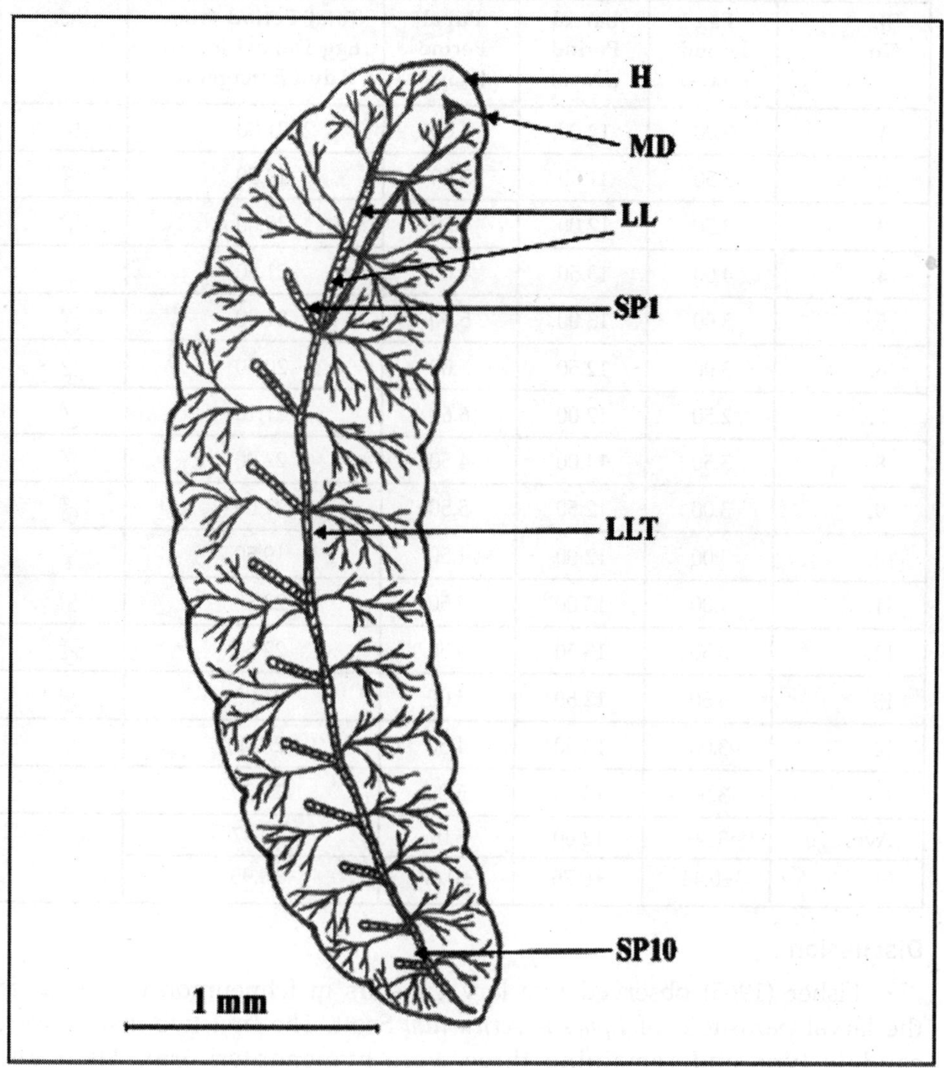

Fig. 4.18b: **Tracheal System of Fourth Instar larva of *X. pedator***

H - Head

MD - Mandible

LL - Loop

LLT - Lateral Longitudinal Trunk

SP1 - First Spiracle

SP10 - Tenth Spiracle

Table 4.2: Developmental period of *G. spodopterae*

Sr. No.	Egg Period (Days)	Larval Period (Days)	Pupal Period (Days)	Total Period from Egg Deposition to Adult Emergence	Sex
1.	3.00	12.00	6.00	21.00	♀
2.	3.50	11.00	5.00	19.50	♂
3.	3.50	12.00	4.50	20.00	♀
4.	4.00	13.50	4.00	21.50	♀
5.	3.00	13.00	5.00	21.00	♂
6.	3.00	12.50	5.00	20.50	♀
7.	2.50	12.00	6.60	21.10	♂
8.	3.50	14.00	4.50	22.00	♂
9.	3.00	12.50	5.50	21.00	♂
10.	3.00	12.00	4.50	19.50	♀
11.	4.00	13.00	5.50	22.50	♀
12.	3.50	13.50	5.50	22.50	♂
13.	3.50	12.50	5.00	21.00	♀
14.	3.00	12.50	4.50	20.00	♀
15.	3.50	13.00	5.00	21.50	♂
Average	3.30	12.60	5.07	20.97	
SE	±0.41	±0.76	±0.67	±0.95	

Discussion

Fisher (1965) observed five larval instars in Ichneumon *C. chlorideae,* the larval parasitoid of *Ephestia sericarium* Scott. The first two instars were caudate type and remaining three were hymenopteriform. Tikar and Thakare (1961) also observed five larval instars in *C. chlorideae,* as internal larval parasitoid of *H. armigera.*

Gangarde (1964) studied the egg structure, immature forms and adults of *C. chlorideae* and observed that *C. chlorideae* have dull white, elongated eggs rounded at both ends. He further reported four instars of parasitoid larvae feeding inside the body of the host. The first instar possessed elongated tail and 13 post embryonic segments. The second instar showed curtailed tail length while third instar exhibited great reduction of last segment.

Table 4.3: Developmental period of *X. pedator*

Sr. No.	Egg Period (Days)	Larval Period (Days)	Pupal Period (Days)	Total Period from Egg Deposition to Adult Emergence	Sex
1.	3.50	8.00	6.00	17.50	♀
2.	4.00	8.50	7.00	19.50	♂
3.	5.00	9.50	6.50	21.00	♂
4.	3.50	12.00	5.50	21.00	♀
5.	4.50	10.00	6.00	20.50	♂
6.	4.50	9.00	5.50	19.00	♀
7.	5.00	10.50	6.00	21.50	♂
8	3.50	12.00	5.50	21.00	♀
9.	4.00	10.50	6.00	20.50	♂
10.	4.00	11.00	5.50	20.50	♀
11.	3.50	9.00	6.00	18.50	♂
12.	5.00	9.50	5.50	20.00	♂
13	4.50	11.50	6.00	22.00	♀
14.	5.00	9.50	6.50	21.00	♀
15.	5.50	11.00	6.00	22.50	♂
Average	4.33	10.10	5.97	20.40	
SE	±0.67	±1.24	±0.44	±1.33	

Fourth instar was comparatively large in size. For emergence from host body the parasitoid thrust its head with pointed mandibles vigorously from venter of the seventh abdominal segment and came out slowly and started construction of their cocoon. The present ichneumonid, *X. pedator* also showed five larval instars with first three caudate and last two hymenopteriform.

Leong and Oatman (1968) studied the biology of *Campoplex haywardi* Blanchard, a solitary internal parasitoid of potato tuber worm *P. operculella,* wherein they reported three larval instars. The larval stages differ in the body form, gross external appearance and mandibular size.

Kajita and Drake (1969) reported the biology of *C. flavipes C. chilonis* the larval parasitoid of *C. suppressalis* and reported three instars in them. The first two were vesiculated type and the third was hymenopteriform. Similarly, Cardona and Oatman (1971) also reported 3 instars in *A. dingus.* Similar result was obtained in the present braconid parasitoid *A. bosei.*

Broodryk (1969) studied the biology of *Chelonus* (*Microchelonus*) *curvimaculatus* Cameron and reported that parasitoid have 3 instars. The first instar possessed the longest period of the larval life and the later instars have taken relatively short period. However, Hamid *et al.* (1970) studied the biology of *Brachycoryphus nursei* (Cameron), parasitoid of the psycid moth, *Clania cameri* Hampson. They found that the parasitoid showed five instars. The entire life cycle required average 15 days (range 9-20 days), average larval period was 6.6 days (range 4-9 days), and average pupal period was 8.6 days (range 3-11 days). The first instar of newly hatched *B. nursei* was sclerotic, light brown and with 13 discrete segments. The gut from the second to 11 segments was clearly visible through the cuticle. Second instar was yellowish in colour and showed all 13 segments of the body. Third fourth and fifth instars were quite similar to each other with cream coloured body, elongate and tapering at both ends.

Cardona and Oatman (1971) studied biology of *A. dingus,* the total developmental period from egg to adult was 18 days. Sathe *et al.* (1987) reported 15 days larval duration in *A. creatonoti,* a larval parasitoid of *T. postica*. In *Apanteles angaleti* Muesebeck and *A. glomeratus* the life cycle were completed in 13.1 and 13.6 days respectively. Oatman and Platner (1974) studied the biology of Ichneumon parasitoid *Temelucha* sp of potato tuber moth *P. operculella*. They reported the immature stages of parasitoid and analyzed 3 larval instars. First instar was with 13 body segments caudate type, second instar was soft and delicate, while third was hymenopteriform and on thirteenth day it emerged from the host and spun its cocoon. In the present ichneumonid, *X. pedator* shows five larval instars; out of which first two were caudate and remaining were hymenopteriform.

Wilson and Ridgway (1975) reported the biology of *Campoletis sonorensis* (Cameron) and found that the parasitoid showed five instars and sex of the parasitoid was apparent in the fourth instar while, in fifth instar clear distinction of sexes was possible, similar results were observed in *Diadegma trichoptilus* (Cameron) by Sathe (1993).

Davaiah *et al.* (1993) reported the life cycle of Indian uzi fly *Exorista bombycis* (Louis.) and reported that the parasitoid completed 5 to 8 generations in a single year; one generation was completed in 15.4 to 50 days varying with the season. The hatching of egg was observed in 1.5 hr to 3-4 days. The larval period was from 4 to 7 days. The pupal duration was from 7 to 8.5 days. The adult longevity of males was 5 to 15 days and for females 20 to 25 days. Similarly, in *C. glomeratus* and *E. bombycis* parasitoids when provided with 10 day old hosts of *Bombyx mori* L. larvae on which the Braconid parasitoid *C. glomeratus* completed the life cycle in 13.1 days while, *E. bombycis* completed the lifecycle within 32.9 days under the laboratory conditions (25±1°C, 60-65 per cent R. H., 12 hr photoperiod) (Sathe and Jadhav, 2001).

The lifecycle studies will be helpful for mass rearing of present parasitoids and in understanding the developmental strategies of parasitoids.

NUTRITION AND ADULT LONGEVITY OF PARASITOIDS

INTRODUCTION

Proper nutritional supply to organisms can enhance their biology and reproductive potential. In short, it is related to metabolic processes and is a connection between ecological and physiological phenomenon concerned with selection and natural competition for food (Gordon, 1962). The biological activities of an organism are dependent on the nutritional requirement and have also connection with environmental factors (Sathe and Margaj, 2001). Nutrition is a major factor which regulates the number of pests as well as biocontrol agents in nature and in the laboratory. According to House (1977), nutrition plays a very significant role in augmentation of biocontrol agents of agricultural pests.

According to Beirne (1962), the nature, quantity and quality of food entirely depend on the effectiveness of biocontrol agents. The failure to identify a suitable supply of food for the biocontrol agents, results into unsuccessful efforts in proper utilization of biological pest control programme. Females of parasitoids require prime source of proteins to produce mature eggs. In nature they get it from honey dew or nectar which contains amino acids. If female fails to get adequate protein nourishment, their eggs get ruptured in the ovarioles and fecundity falls which might greatly hamper the biological control programme (Srivastava, 1996). For mass rearing of parasitoids in the polyhouse or rearing unit flowering plants may be adequately planted for fulfilling the nutritional requirement of parasitoids. The nutritional requirement of biocontrol agents are not fully studied so far and hence considered as the prime area of research. Keeping in the view, the significance of nutritional requirement in improving the role of parasitoids in pest management, the present work was carried out.

Materials and Methods

The laboratory reared parasitoids were used for the analysis of nutritional requirement. In the test tube, size 20×2.8 cm, parasitoids were taken and 100 per cent honey, 50 per cent honey, 10 per cent honey, 50 per cent sucrose, 50 per cent glucose, apple fruit juice, citrus fruit juice and water were provided separately to them. In control, adults were starved, given no water and food. The feed was changed twice in a day with cotton soaked food material. The observations and cleaning were made at 12 hour interval under laboratory conditions (25±2°C, 65±5% R.H.). Each experiment was replicated 5 times.

Results

A. bosei

The results recorded in Table 4.4 and Fig. 4.22 indicated that, the mean longevity of males when fed with 50 per cent sucrose, 50 per cent glucose and 10 per cent honey averaged 5.4, 5.2 and 7.6 days and that of females 6.6, 6.4 and 8.6 days respectively. Neither of sex survived for more than 2 days without food. The 100 per cent honey showed maximum adult longevity with 10.8 and 12.2 days for males and females respectively and 50 per cent honey exhibited 9.8 days for males and 12.6 days for females but comparing to these, 50 per cent honey showed maximum longevity ratio for male to female (1:1.28). The ratio of adult longevity was favoring the longevity of females hence, it could be best suited feed for in-vitro rearing of *A. bosei*. With apple fruit juice and citrus fruit juice the longevity of males and females averaged 3.6, 4.6 days and 4.4, 5.2 days respectively. In control, no parasitoid could survive for more than 2 days.

G. spodopterae

The results represented in Table 4.5 and Fig. 4.23 showed that, in control both the sexes survived for not more than 2 days. Mean longevity of males averaged 7.4, 6.4 and 6.6 days and females 8.8, 7.0 and 7.2 days when fed with 10 per cent honey, 50 per cent sucrose and 50 per cent glucose respectively. While, longevity of males averaged 11.6, 9.2 days and females 14.2, 10.4 days when fed with 100 per cent honey and 50 per cent honey respectively. There was no significant difference in the longevity of both sexes when fed with apple fruit juice and citrus fruit juice. The mean longevity ratio for male to female showed higher when parasitoid was fed with 100 per cent honey (1:1.22) hence, it was best suited feed for maintaining laboratory culture of *G. spodopterae*.

X. pedator

The results tabulated in Table 4.6 and Fig. 4.24 indicated that both sexes have showed longevity of 1-2 days and with water it was of 2-4 days. The male adult longevity averaged 19.0, 15.2, 10.8, 8.0, 6.0, 5.8 and 4.2 days and female longevity averaged 21.8, 18.4, 12.0, 9.0, 6.8, 6.6 and 4.2 days with 100 per cent honey, 50 per cent honey, 10 per cent honey, 50 per cent sucrose, 50 per cent glucose, apple fruit juice and citrus fruit juice respectively. Similar to *A. bosei*, *X. pedator* also revealed maximum longevity ratio with 50 per cent honey offered as feed with ratio, 1:1.21. Therefore, 50 per cent honey could be best suited feed for in-vitro rearing of *X. pedator*.

Table 4.4: Nutritional requirement of *A. bosei*.

Food Supplied	Sex	Longevity (Days)		Mean Longevity Ratio (♂:♀)
		Range	Mean±SE	
100% honey	Male	10–12	10.8±0.83	1 : 1.13
	Female	10–13	12.9±1.30	
50% honey	Male	9–11	9.8±0.83	1 : 1.29
	Female	11–14	12.6±1.14	
10% honey	Male	6–9	7.6±1.14	1 : 1.13
	Female	7–10	8.6±1.14	
50% sucrose	Male	5–6	5.4±0.55	1 : 1.22
	Female	6–8	6.6±0.89	
50% glucose	Male	4–7	5.2±1.30	1 : 1.23
	Female	4–8	6.4±1.67	
Apple fruit juice	Male	3–5	3.6±0.89	1 : 1.22
	Female	4–5	4.4±0.54	
Citrus fruit juice	Male	4–6	4.8±0.84	1 : 1.08
	Female	3–7	5.2±1.48	
Water	Male	1–2	1.4±0.55	1 : 1
	Female	1–2	1.4±0.54	
Control	Male	1–2	1.2±0.45	1 : 1
	Female	1–2	1.2±0.44	

Table 4.5: Nutritional requirement of *G. spodopterae*.

Food Supplied	Sex	Longevity (Days)		Mean Longevity Ratio (♂:♀)
		Range	Mean±SE	
1	2	3		4
100% honey	Male	10–13	11.6±1.14	1 : 1.22
	Female	13–15	14.2±0.84	
50% honey	Male	8–10	9.2±0.84	1 : 1.13
	Female	9–12	10.4±1.34	
10% honey	Male	6–8	7.4±0.89	1 : 1.19
	Female	8–10	8.8±1.10	
50% sucrose	Male	5–8	6.4±1.14	1 : 1.09
	Female	5–9	7.0±1.58	

Contd...

1	2	3		4
50% glucose	Male	5–8	6.6±1.14	1 : 1.09
	Female	6–9	7.2±1.30	
Apple fruit juice	Male	4–6	5.0±0.71	1 : 1.16
	Female	5–7	5.8±0.83	
Citrus fruit juice	Male	4–6	4.8±0.84	1 : 1.16
	Female	5–7	5.6±1.14	
Water	Male	1–2	1.4±0.55	1 : 1.14
	Female	1–2	1.6±0.54	
Control	Male	1–2	1.2±0.44	1 : 1
	Female	1–2	1.2±0.44	

Table 4.6: Nutritional requirement of *X. pedator*.

Food Supplied	Sex	Longevity (Days)		Mean Longevity Ratio (♂:♀)
		Range	Mean±SE	
100% honey	Male	17–21	19.0±1.41	1 : 1.15
	Female	19–24	21.8±1.72	
50% honey	Male	14–17	15.2±1.16	1 : 1.21
	Female	16–20	18.4±1.62	
10% honey	Male	10–12	10.8±0.84	1 : 1.11
	Female	10–14	12.0±1.58	
50% sucrose	Male	7–9	8.0±0.89	1 : 1.13
	Female	8–10	9.0±0.63	
50% glucose	Male	5–7	6.0±1.00	1 : 1.13
	Female	6–8	6.8±0.74	
Apple fruit juice	Male	5–7	5.8±0.83	1 : 1.14
	Female	5–8	6.6±1.01	
Citrus fruit juice	Male	3–5	4.2±0.74	1 : 1
	Female	3–6	4.2±1.16	
Water	Male	2–4	2.8±0.74	1 : 1.07
	Female	2–4	3.0±0.63	
Control	Male	1–2	1.6±0.48	1 : 1
	Female	1–2	1.6±0.48	

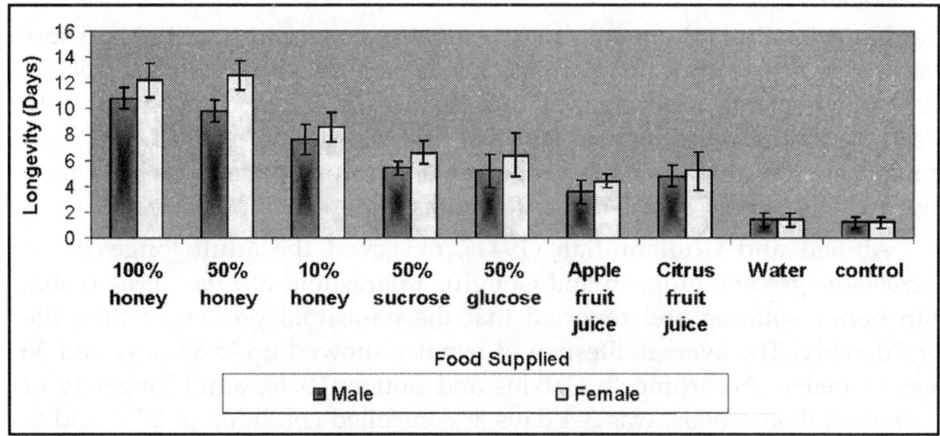

Fig. 4.22: **Nutritional requirement of *A. bosei.***

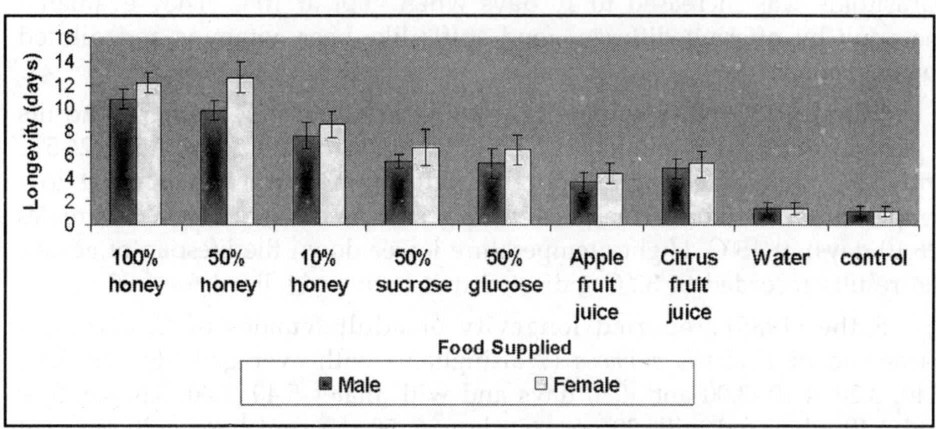

Fig. 4.23: **Nutritional requirement of *G. spodopterae.***

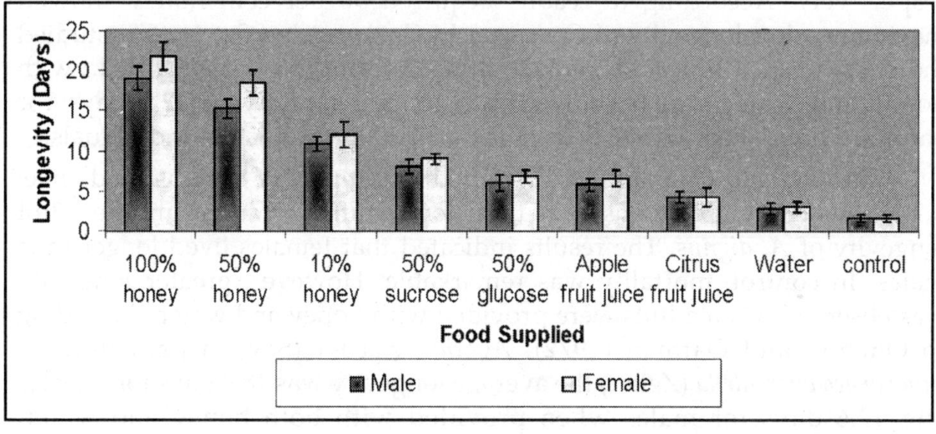

Fig. 4.24: **Nutritional requirement of *X. pedator.***

Discussion

Nutritional requirements are investigated in several parasitoids. There was evidence that intricate relations exist between insects, their food plants and the associated biocontrol agents (House, 1977). According to Smith (1957), sex ratio, reproduction, survival and size of the females compared to males varied in several species of hymenopterous parasitoids with their host and nutritional supplements for parasitoids.

Ahmed and Ghulamullah (1941), observed the adult longevity in *Microbracon greeni* (Dudgeon and Gough), a parasitoid of *Erias vitella* (Fab.), with honey solution and reported that the parasitoid prolonged their life considerably. The average lifespan of females showed up to 53 days and 36 days in males. According to Calkins and Sutter (1976), adult longevity of *Apanteles militaris* Wals. was 3-4 days at controlled condition of 27°C and 6-7 days when they were fed with diluted honey solutions. The longevity of parasitoids was increased to 10 days when kept at 10°C. They evaluated the adult by offering different food stuffs like beer, vitamins and diluted sugar solution, etc.

Broodryk (1969) examined *Chelonus curvimaculatus* Cameron adults separately at different temperature ranges varied from 2°C, 12°C, 15°C, 26.5°C and 32°C. These tests resulted that adult longevity enhances at low temperature. The adult females lived longer (46.54 days) at 11°C while males (26.10 days) at 15°C. Higher temperature lower down the lifespan of adults, the results recorded at 32°C indicated that both sexes lived for 1.50 days.

Sathe (1985), reported longevity of adult females of *C. diurnii*, a parasitoid of *Exelastis atomosa* (Walsingham) with averaged lifespan 5.40, 7.40, 3.20, 4.40, 3.00 and 4.20 days and with males 5.40, 7.60, 3.6, 4.6, 3.20 and 4.40 when fed with 20 per cent honey, 50 per cent honey, 20 per cent glucose, 50 per cent glucose, 20 per cent sucrose and 50 per cent sucrose respectively. According to results acquired 50 per cent honey showed maximum adult longevity of *C. diurnii*. In *C. glomeratus*, Sato (1975) studied the survival of a braconid parasitoid at 23°C and 58 per cent R.H., with honey and water which showed maximum longevity of 22.9 days for naturally nourished and 26.5 days for artificially nourished individuals.

Cardona and Oatman (1971) studied the impact of various foods like: honey, water, combinations of natural food stuffs for analyzing the adult longevity of *A. dignus*. The results indicated that females lived longer than males. In control, mortality was remarkable. However, greater longevity was observed when adults were provided with honey and water. According to Odebiyi and Oatman (1972), *Agathis gibbosa* (Say), a parasitoid of *Pthorimaea operculella* (Zeller) the average longevity was 18.0 days for females and 12.6 days for males when provided with both honey and water. Similarly, they also reported that the females lived longer than males.

Kajita and Drake (1969) studied *C. chilonis* and *C. flavipes* with the influence of certain foodstuff combinations on the longevity of adults and found decreased longevity in both parasitoids when fed with water and enhanced when diluted honey was supplied. Likely, Hidaka (1965) also reported adult longevity of *C. chilonis* and found that under natural conditions the adults could survive for an average 5.10 days when fed with diluted honey. With the help of water, honey and sugar solutions, Oatman *et al.* (1969) increased adult lifespan of *Orgilus lepidus* Mueseback. They also found that adults survived for 3-5 days in the absence of food and water and lived longer when provided both honey and water. They reported average longevity of males 23.9 days and for females 21.4 days. In the present study the parasitoids did not survived for more than 2 days without food, the maximum survival was noted of 12.9 days, 21.8 days and 14.2 days for females and 10.8 days, 19.0 days and 11.6 days for males when given 100 per cent honey solution.

MATING BEHAVIOUR

INTRODUCTION

Insects are the largest group of animals; they reveal a variety of courtship patterns. The term mating behaviour tends to the behavioural events surrounding towards insemination, which help for successful sperm transfer by the male and taken up by the female as well. Mating behaviour is most important of all the activities performed by animal in the sexual reproduction (Martins, 1971). According to Dowell and Horn (1975), mating and pest management has direct relationship hence, mating is an important component of pest control.

The mating behaviour in insects can typically involve series of mating steps (Bousch and Baerwald, 1967; Cole, 1970). Mating behaviour may differ among the insect species or even in between two sexes of same species. Some insects are polygamous in which mating occurred several times whereas, some are monogamous in which mating occurred only once and they are capable to produce the eggs (Srivastava, 1996). According to Simmonds (1963) the mating behaviour of an insect can directly influence the biocontrol programme as well as genetic control of insect pests. Since, mating of a pest and parasitoid has a great importance for controlling of the target species and hence they are widely studied in many cases (Atkins, 1980). Review of literature indicates that parasitoid courtship and mating behaviour in parasitic hymenoptera have been attempted by several workers. Noteworthy among them refer to Cardona and Oatman (1971), Sathe, (1985), Sathe and Nikam (1983, 1984), Sathe (1986a), Beukeboom and Assem (2001) etc.

According to King and Radchiffe (1969), fertilization is mandatory for the production of the females in parasitic wasps. During copulation, male products are introduced into a female's genital tract by means of sexual contact and the sperms are stored in the spermatheca until required for fertilization.

Bastock (1967) reported that, the potentially immature females do not allow copulation rather males have to induce excitement to copulate by means of some sort of efforts which are in sequential manner and may be called as courtship behaviour. According to Borgia (1979) multiple copulation plays a vital role enhancing the reproductive potential of parasitoid females (Thornhill and Alcock, 1983). According to van den Assem (1986) parasitoid females utilize sperms of a second male for enhancing the reproductive rate. According to Raulston *et al.* (1976) realized that, the mating behaviour of adult parasitoids in the field and laboratory conditions are of great concern to the physiologists and pest management researchers. In the present investigation, mating behaviours of three hymenopterous parasitoids namely: *A. bosei, G. spodopterae* and *X. pedator* have been studied.

Materials and Methods

The mating behaviour of *A. bosei, G. spodopterae* and *X. pedator* were studied by using laboratory reared parasitoids of both sexes (25±2°C temperature, 62±5 per cent R.H., and 12 hr photoperiod). Newly emerged parasitoid pair (♂ and ♀) was confined in separate test tube (size 20×2.8cm) and pre-mating, mating and post-mating behaviour have been noted. The parasitoids preference towards food was also recorded by spot observations. To study mating interruptions, one female was kept along with five males in a single test tube. During the experiment the adults of both sexes were fed with 50 per cent honey. The following behaviour was noted in parasitoids.

- *Pre-mating phase:* The period ranges between the emergence of adult and starting of courtship behaviour.
- *Mating phase:* The mating phase referred to the starting of courtship behaviour of parasitoid to the termination of coitous.
- *Post-mating phase:* The stage from the termination of coitous to the death of parasitoid.
- *High phase:* The male hold its head away from the female dorsum and vibrates the wings aggressively over a high frequency simultaneously performing a sort of movement with its hind legs on the female wings.
- *Low phase:* The wings are kept steady and remain elevated whereas, the hind legs are kept in the place. The male curves the entire body in such a way that the head comes near to the female thorax and concurrently he presses the tip of its gaster on the upper side of the female wings.

Results

1. Mating Behaviour of *A. bosei* (Plate 4, Figs. 25 to 28)

Pre-mating

The average premating period was 32.5 min (Table 4.7). During the premating phase there was no excitation behaviour between the male and female. The newly emerged species spend the time for cleaning of their body but did not perform any excitation related to mating. The males were more active than females and both are attracted towards the food (50% honey).

Mating

When a pair (♂ and ♀) was placed in a test tube, immediately male responded to attraction behaviour and recognized the female by excitements through recognition behaviour (Fig. 4.25). Orientation, wing vibration (fanning) and antennation (Fig. 4.26) was carried out by the males for approaching the females. When female remain steady, the male attempted for touching the abdomen by its antennae. This activity carried out for 10-15 min and mounting was attempted. Mounting of males consisted of low phase, pause phase and high phase in sequential manner and it takes on an average 2.5 min, 1 min and 1.5 min respectively.

Female Acceptance Behaviour

Female demonstrated subsequent series of behaviours:

Remain steady, antennae holding, abdomen cleaning, wing spreading, ovipositor extrusion and genital spreading.

Female Repelling Behaviour

Female demonstrated subsequent series of behaviours:

Kicking, escaping, decamping, wings fluttering, abdomen elevation, depression and extrusion.

The male followed the female with earlier wing fluttering and later with wings elevation. For a while, male tapped the thorax and abdomen of female with its antennae and mounted the female from the side. While holding female, the male slanted its body, so that female head was pointed in the same direction. Male mounted (Fig. 4.27) a female with the head towards the female abdomen but rapidly changed the direction. The male instantly moved back, bend his abdomen down and copulated with female (Fig. 4.28). The copulation lasted for 30 sec (range 25-35 sec). The high phase, pause and low phase averaged 4.5 sec, 1.5 sec and 3.5 sec respectively.

The pair remained stationary during copulation. Males were polygamous whereas, females were monogamous. The female on an average was receptive for 4 days (range 2.5 to 4.5 days) after the emergence. More than one male exposed in test tube resulted in to disturbance in copulation.

The average mating period was 4.5 min (range 3 to 5 min). It was observed that during the mating period both sexes were not attracted towards the food (50 % honey).

Post-mating

After mating, the female could not show receptivity and no mating was performed by the female while, male showed grooming behaviour and mated with newly introduced females. During post mating both sexes moved away and remains stationary. The pair after mating immediately attracted towards the food. The average post mating period was 7.50 days (range 6.0 to 8.0 days).

2. Mating Behaviour of *G. spodopterae* (Plate 5, Figs. 4.29 to 4.32)

Pre-mating

Pre-mating period in *G. spodopterae* was 28 min (25 min-32 min) (Table 4.7). Both sexes were engaged in cleaning their body and no excitement was shown by either male or female and both were attracted towards the food.

Mating

Mating occurred after 5 hours from emergence, excitation was shown by both sexes. Mating was observed at day time. Attraction, recognition (Fig. 4.29), orientation, antennae tapping, wing vibration, wing fluking, leg vibration, grooming, cleaning of abdomen, antennation (Fig. 4.30) and mounting (Fig. 4.31 and 4.32) steps were performed during the mating behaviour.

Female Acceptance Behaviour

Receptive female showed following series of behaviours:

Remain steady, spreading wings, antennae holding, abdomen cleaning, wing spreading, ovipositor extrusion and genital spreading.

Female Repelling Behaviour

Non receptive female demonstrated subsequent series of behaviours:

Kicking, escaping, decamping, wings fluttering, abdomen elevation, depression and extrusion.

The copulation phase lasted for an average of 30 sec (range 26-33 sec). The coitous was terminated by male. Males were polygamous while females were monogamous. Presence of more than one male interrupted copulation. The average period of high phase, pause and low phase were 4 sec, 1.5 sec and 3 sec respectively.

Post-mating

During the postmating period both sexes were attracted towards the food. Females were not receptive to males but males showed antennae orientation, abdomen movement and grooming for mating. The average post mating period was 6.5 days.

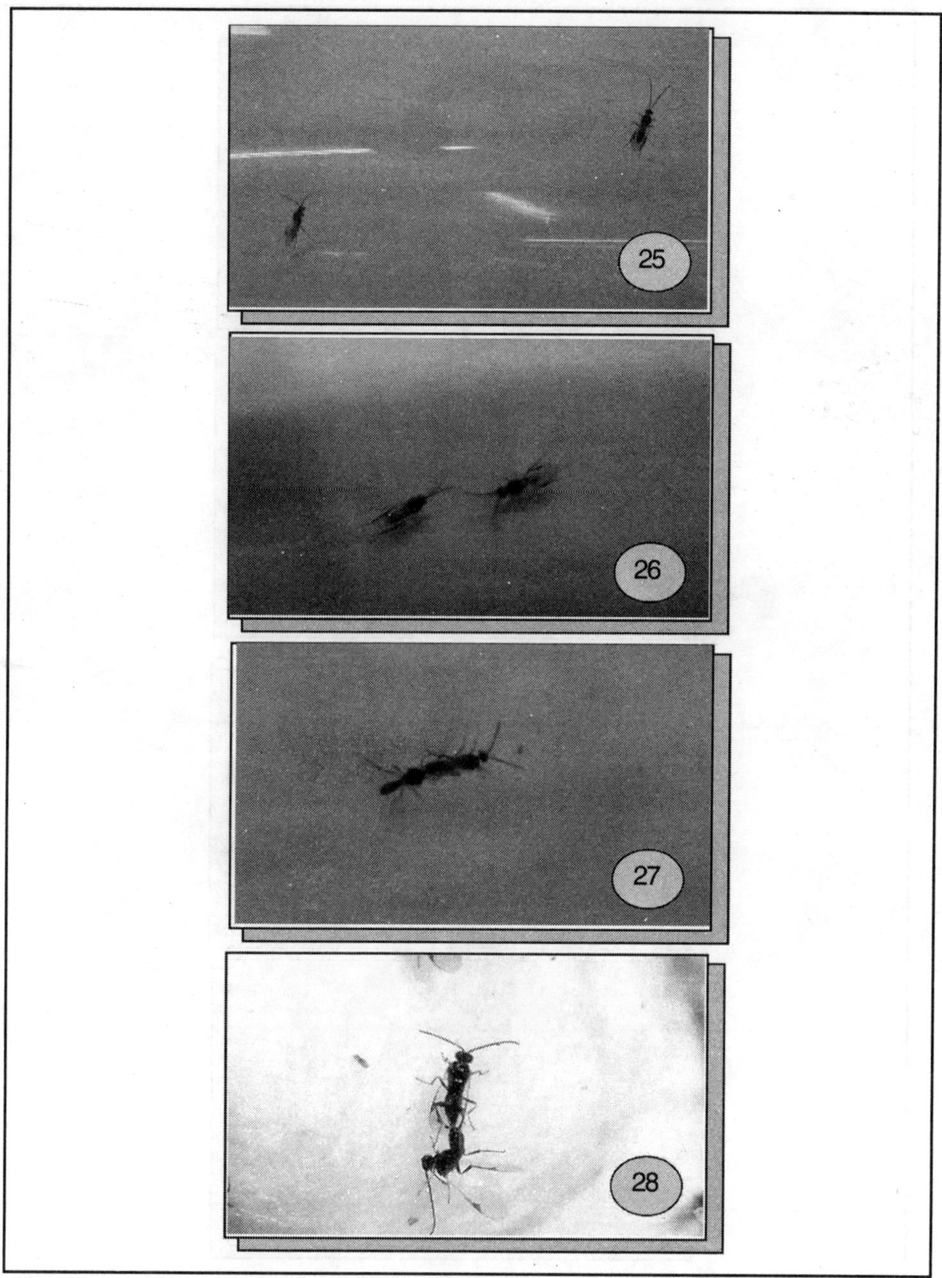

Plage - 4 (Figs. 25-28): ***A. bosei:* Mating Behaviour.** Fig. 4.25: **Recognition,** Fig. 4.26: **Antennation,** Fig. 4.27: **Mounting,** Fig. 4.28: **Copulation**

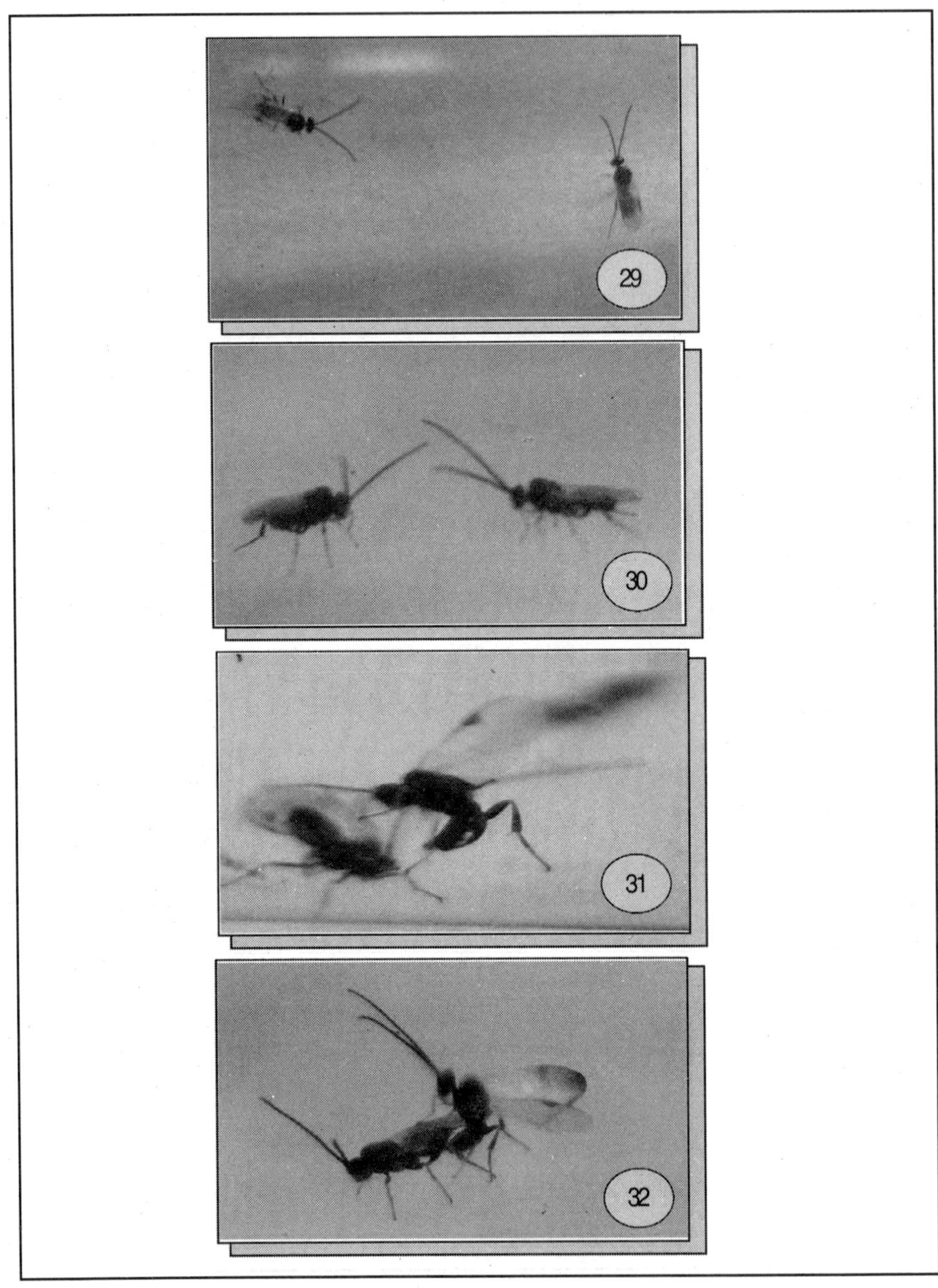

Plage - 5 (Figs. 29-32): ***G. spodopterae:*** **Mating Behaviour.** Fig. 4.29: **Recognition,** Fig. 4.30: **Antennation,** Fig. 4.31: **Mounting,** Fig. 4.32: **Copulation**

3. Mating Behaviour of *X. pedator* (Plate 6, Figs. 4.33 to 4.36)

Pre-mating

During this phase males demonstrated exciting behaviours through wing fanning, orientation of antennae and cleaning of abdomen etc. Both sexes were attracted towards the food during the premating period. Pre-mating phase lasts for 5 hr (4.5 hr-6.5 hr) (Table 4.7).

Mating

Mating was recorded for 30 min. and it was observed during day time. Males performed different steps of courtship behaviours like: orientation, recognition (Fig. 4.33), antennation (Fig. 4.34), wing fanning, abdomen cleaning, grooming and mounting (Fig. 4.35).

Female Acceptance Behaviour

Female showed following steps:

Remain steady, antennae holding, abdomen cleaning, wing spreading, ovipositor extrusion and genital spreading.

Female Repelling Behaviour

Non receptive female demonstrated subsequent series of behaviours:

Kicking, escaping, decamping, wings fluttering, abdomen elevation, depression and extrusion.

Male hold its antennae at 60° angle and tapped the antennae to the receptive female and mounted the female. The average period of high phase, pause and low phase were 5 sec, 2 sec, 3 sec respectively. The male hold the thorax of female with his legs and then arched the abdomen to copulate the female (Fig. 4.36). The pair remained immobile during copulation. The copulation period was 35 sec (range 31-38 sec). If more than one male present, mating and copulation interrupted. The females were monogamous but, males were polygamous.

Post-mating

After mating both the sexes were attracted towards food. During post mating period male showed antennae orientation, abdomen movement and walking towards female for mating but female responded negatively to avoid mounting. The average post mating period was 8 days.

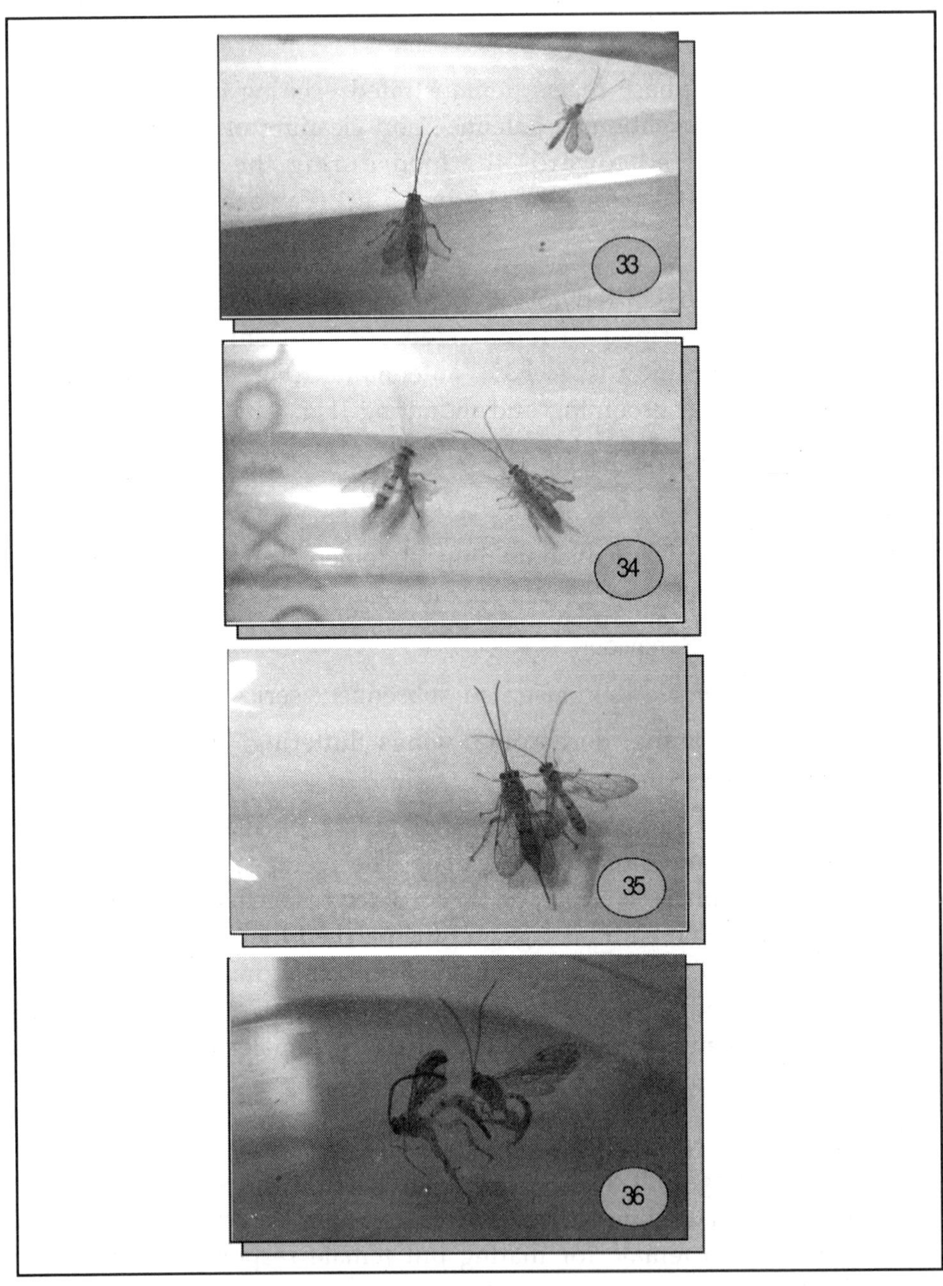

Plage - 6 (Figs. 33-36): ***X. pedator:* Mating Behaviour.** Fig. 4.33: **Recognition,** Fig. 4.34: **Antennation,** Fig. 4.35: **Mounting,** Fig. 4.36: **Copulation**

Table 4.7: Mating behaviour of parasitoids

Observations	*A. bosei*	*G. spodopterae*	*X. pedator*
Average Pre-mating period	32.5 min	28 min	5 hr
Mating	Mate 2-3 times in a day	Mate 2-3 times in a day	Mate 3-5 times in a day
Average copulation period	30 sec	30 sec	5-7 min
Average Post-mating period	7.5 days	6.5 days	8 days
Attraction after mating (male, female)	Attracted towards food	Attracted towards food	Attracted towards food
Mating occurred at	Day	Day	Both day and night

Discussion

According to Sathe and Margaj (2001), braconid parasitoids typically perform following mating behavioural pattern *viz;* attraction, recognition, orientation, wing fanning, antennation, mounting, copulation and post copulatory grooming. They studied *A. earterus, A. pectinophorae, A. pusaensis* wherein the premating period was 30 min., 20 min. and 25 min. respectively. Laing and Caltagirone (1969), stated that the premating period is the characteristics of species in hymenopteran parasitoids, but most of species mate immediately after emergence from cocoons. According to Oatman *et al.* (1969), braconid parasitoids *O. lepidus* and *P. dignus* does not showed premating period. They were parasitoid of potato tuber worm *Keiferia lycopersicella* (Walsingham). In present findings *A. bosei, G. spodopterae* and *X. pedator* showed averaged premating period of 3 hr, 28 min and 6 hr respectively.

According to Weseloh (1977) females of *Cotesia* (=*Apanteles*) *melanoscelus* Ratzeburg, a solitary larval braconid parasitoid of gypsy moth *Lymantria dispar* (L.) remain receptive towards males for at least 11 days of their adult life and were mated. Similarly, he also reported the courtship pattern of *A. melanoscelus,* consisted a number of stereotyped elements including wing elevation, fluttering and extreme fluttering occurred before mating. Copulation occurred immediately after mounting, male responded to female under a variety of conditions but female determined the mating success. Virgin parasitoid females released in the mating chamber were not disturbed to previously mated females and permitted males to mate for more times.

According to Odebiyi and Oatman (1972) in *A. gibbosa* a parasitoid of *P. operculella* excitement at sexes was noted when caged in the mating chamber. In presences of the female, the male bend the tip of the abdomen downward and fanned its wings and pursued the female which tried to escape. After several attempts male eventually caught the female and grasped with legs. The ovipositor moved aside and the male bent the tip of the abdomen downward to insert the aedeagus into the female genital track. The pair remained stationary during copulation. They recorded observations of 24 pairs and found that, the copulation was lasted for 25 to 95 sec (average 55 sec).

OVIPOSITION BEHAVIOUR

INTRODUCTION

Oviposition behaviour involves number of qualitative and quantitative factors (Similowitz and Iwantsch, 1975). The success of oviposition depends on habitat selection, host acceptance and ability of parasitization by the parasitoids (Herrebout, 1969). Oviposition is the practical phenomenon on which the success of biocontrol programme is dependent. According to Mathews (1974) and Salt (1935a) the ovipositing females search for particular habitat before attracted towards potent host. The females of many parasitoids locate hosts by indiscriminate wandering until hosts are observed at very short range through the antennal contact (Hafeez, 1961). Parasitoids lay their eggs inside the body of host whereas, the predators on the locality of the host *i.e.,* away from the body of host in which after hatching from eggs the predators find their host. However, some tachinids parasitoids lay their eggs on host plants instead of host body (Sathe, 2014). Some Hymenopterous parasitoids, avoid parasitism on previously parasitized host but some cannot discriminate hosts those are already parasitized (Sathe 1986b, Barren and Boivin 1998, Sathe 2014, 2015).

Review of literature indicates that Ayyar and Narayanswami (1940), Nishida (1956), Nobel and Graham (1966), Matthews (1974), Leong and Oatman (1968).

Sathe and Nikam (1983, 1984), Sathe and Bhosale (1996), Sathe and Margaj (1996, 2001), Sathe (2014), Sathe (2015) etc., worked on oviposition behaviours in parasitic hymenoptera.

Materials and Methods

The newly mated females of parasitoids were confined in the test tubes or glass cage (Fig. 4.37-4.39) along with their appropriate hosts and oviposition behaviour was observed. 3-5 day old larvae of *A. moorei*, 4-6 day old larvae of *S. litura* and 3-4 day old pupae of *C. partellus* were exposed to the females of *A. bosei*, *G. spodopterae* and *X. pedator* respectively. Respective host plants were also confining in the oviposition unit for studying pre oviposition, oviposition and post oviposition behaviour of parasitoids. Ten parasitoid females were attempted in the laboratory for study of oviposition behaviour.

Following aspects of oviposition have been taken into account

Pre Oviposition Period

The period between emergence of female and initiate excitement for oviposition.

Oviposition Period

The period from beginning of female excitement up to completion of oviposition.

Post Oviposition Period

The period between completion of oviposition till the death of female.

Ovipositional Attack

The time at which actual insertion of the ovipositor takes place in to the host species.

Results

1. Oviposition Behaviour of *A. bosei* (Plate 7, Fig. 4.37)

Oviposition behaviour of *A. bosei* is recorded in Table 4.8 and Fig. 4.37.

Pre oviposition

A. bosei females were attracted towards food during pre oviposition period. Females after exposure of host showed no excitement, remained steady and refused the hosts for oviposition. The averaged pre oviposition period was 32.5 min (range 29 to 34 min).

Oviposition

During oviposition period females showed antennal orientation. They were quite active and walked on the damaged host plant leaves by tapping the surface with antennae. While contacting damaged area of leaf, female remains steady and make circular grooming movements. Female examined the host larva and within few seconds oviposited on the host (Fig. 4.37). 3-5 days old host larvae were preferred for oviposition. The oviposition period averaged 3 sec (range 1 to 4 sec).

Post oviposition

During post oviposition period females did not execute any kind of movement pertaining to oviposition. Females remained stationary and inactive even after host larva came closer, female moved away and remain still at the corner of petri plate. Female get attracted towards feed, 50 per cent honey. The average post oviposition period was 3 days (range 2 to 4 days).

2. Oviposition Behaviour of *G. spodopterae* (Plate 7, Fig. 4.38)

The results of oviposition behaviour of *G. spodopterae* are recorded in Table 4.8 and Fig. 4.38.

Pre oviposition

The averaged pre oviposition period recorded was 27 min (range 23 to 28 min). Females were attracted towards food (100% honey) during pre oviposition period and have not shown any excitement even after exposure of *S. litura* caterpillar. The female did not perform any oviposition behaviour during this period.

Oviposition

Females performed rapid search for hosts by moving antennae through antennal orientation. The oviposition was stimulated by the presence of damaged host plant parts. After contacting the host, female oviposited quickly within 3 sec. Female deposited the eggs through the oviposition attack with ovipositor which was located at the last abdominal segment. The females might be attracted towards the host haemolymph oozed out from the host body due to wound formed by the ovipositor. However, females feed on the 100 per cent honey after and before oviposition period. The average oviposition period was 5.5 days (range 4 to 6 days).

Post oviposition

Post oviposition period averaged 5 (range 3 to 6) days. The presence of *S. litura* caterpillar as host not stimulated female for oviposition. The female remained away from the host in glass cage. During the post oviposition period females were given 100 per cent honey as a feed.

3. Oviposition behaviour of *X. pedator* (Plate 7, Fig. 4.39)

The results of oviposition behaviour of *X. pedator* are recorded in Table 4.8 and Fig. 4.39.

Pre-oviposition

The averaged pre oviposition period of *X. pedator* was 36.5 min (range 34 to 37 min). Females were given 50 per cent honey as a feed and female dose not showed any response towards the host during oviposition.

Oviposition

Females performed exciting behaviours when jowar stem along with host larvae were exposed. The female moved closer towards the stem by tapping the surface through antennae. After reaching to the frass of host larvae, female performed rapid searching behaviour, thereby thrusting the ovipositor into the frass and quickly deposited the egg (oviposition period 15 min). If failed to locate the pupa, female searched for another stem or different site on the stem available. Exposed host pupa could be immediately parasitized by the female.

Plage - 7 (Figs. 37-39): **Oviposition Behaviour.** Fig. 4.37: ***A. bosei***, Fig. 4.38: ***G. spodopterae***, Fig. 4.39: ***X. pedator***

The parasitoids followed chain of oviposition behaviour: attraction towards host, recognition, antennal examination, upward and downward movements of abdomen, thrusting of ovipositor, insertion of ovipositor and actual oviposition. The same chain of behaviour was found in all three parasitoids studied.

Post oviposition

During post oviposition period female could not performed any sort of movements of oviposition. Females remain inactive. They remain stationary at one side of cage. However, during the course they were attracted towards 50 per cent honey as feed. The average post oviposition period was 6 (range 3 to 8) days.

Table 4.8: Oviposition behaviour of parasitoids

Observation Parameters	*A. bosei*	*G. spodopterae*	*X. pedator*
Pre oviposition period	32.30 min	27 min	36.30 min
Oviposition period	3 sec	3 sec	15 min
Oviposition days	5 days	5.5 days	6.5 days
Post oviposition period	3 days	5 days	6 days
Feeding before and after Oviposition	Feed on 50% honey	Feed on 50% honey	Feed on 50% honey
Oviposition stimulant	Damaged sorghum leaf and ear head	Damaged soybean pods and scraped leaves by larvae	Damaged jowar stem with frass

Discussion

Oviposition behaviour in parasitoids could be helpful for the successful mass culture of parasitoid. In *Opilus lepidus*, the braconid larval parasitoid of the potato tuber worm *P. operculella* showed shorter pre oviposition period and female quickly oviposited in to the host (Oatman *et al.* 1969). Similarly, Nishida (1956) reported the pre oviposition period as 3 days for *O. fletcheri*, an endoparasitoid of melon fruit fly *Dacus cucurbitae* Coquillet. While, the females of *C. curvimaculatus*, the braconid larval parasitoid of potato tuber worm *P. operculella*, the parasitoid deposited their eggs as soon as the host was exposed in the rearing unit (Broodryk, 1969). According to Cardona and Oatman (1971), the pre oviposition period was 80 sec of *A. dignus*, the solitary larval parasitoid of *K. lycopersicella*. While in the present findings the pre oviposition periods were 32.30 min, 27 min and 36.30 min for *A. bosei*, *G. spodopterae* and *X. pedator* respectively.

Cardona and Oatman (1971) also studied oviposition and post oviposition behaviour of *A. dignus*. They reported that the change in texture of the leaf and mined area plays very crucial role in oviposition. Female critically inspected the infested area and located the optimum position of host caterpillar. Afterwards, the females rapidly thrust the ovipositor for finding the host and if failed to locate the host caterpillar the female removed the ovipositor and searched for the new place. Sathe and Margaj (2001) studied the females of *A. earterus, A. pectinophorae* and *A. pusaensis* which showed excitements, extensive searching and thrusting of ovipositor in to the cotton balls which were damaged by bollworms before actual oviposition into the host species.

According to Odebiyi and Oatman (1972), the females of *A. gibbosa* insert its ovipositor into the larval frass and locate the host by making several attempts. In *A. oblique* the larval parasitoid of *S. obliqua*, the female parasitoid exhibited the chain of behaviours like: attraction of host, recognition, examination through antennae, upward and downward movement of abdomen, thrusting of ovipositor, insertion of ovipositor and actual oviposition in the host body. The same steps have been noted in the present parasitoids *A. bosei, G. spodopterae* and *X. pedator*. In several host parasitoid models above said steps are noted (Sathe and Nikam, 1983, 1984; Sathe, 1990; Sathe and Bhosale, 1996; Sathe and Margaj, 2001; Sathe 2014, 2015).

Feeding of females on 50 per cent honey during oviposition was observed in all parasitoid studied however no attraction has been noticed towards the host haemolymph oozed out of host species. However, some ichneumons like: *C. chlorideae* and *E. argenteopilosus* were found to feed on haemolymph oozed out at the time of oviposition as reported by Sathe and Shanthakumar (1992), Quednau and Guevremont (1975) and Sathe (1990).

Cardona and Oatman (1971) reported average post oviposition period as 3 days in *A. dignus*. In *C. haywardi* the post oviposition period noticed as long as 21 days, whereas shortest post oviposition period was 1 day (Leong and Oatman, 1968). According to Broodryk (1969), in *C. curvimaculatus* the post oviposition period maximized for 28 days. However, according to Doutt (1947) in many parasitoid post oviposition period was not observed. In present findings, the post oviposition period averaged 3, 5 and 6 days for *A. bosei, G. spodopterae* and *X. pedator* respectively under laboratory conditions (25±2°C, 60±5 per cent R.H., and 12 hr photoperiod).

The present work will enhance the understanding of oviposition behaviour of parasitoids and mass rearing of biocontrol agents. The shorter pre oviposition period, longer oviposition period, quick oviposition attack, high searching capacity, etc., are important characteristics of an ideal parasitoid. Therefore, the present work will help for providing baseline data for mass rearing of above three parasitoids.

Reproductive Potential of Parasitoids

HOST DENSITY SELECTION

INTRODUCTION

Optimum host density for parasitization is crucial aspect for mass rearing of parasitoids (Sathe and Margaj, 2001). In fact the searching and selection of host density by the parasitoid counts the success of biocontrol programme of any pest species. Host density dependent factor for host parasitoid model suggest the number of parasitoids to be released in the field to control the pest population. The density of hosts may vary the parasitism potential of parasitoids. The optimum host density boosts the per cent parasitism of parasitoids, which ultimately enhance the biocontrol programme. The in-vitro study of parasitoids depends on the density of hosts exposed and proper food supplement to the parasitoids. The optimum host density increases the biocontrol potential of parasitoids and possesses prime importance in laboratory culture of parasitoids and efficient production of mass culture of parasitoids to control the pest population in the field (Nikam and Basarkar 1981, Sathe 2014, 2015).

Review of literature indicates that Khan and Verma (1945), Oatman *et al.* (1969), Cardona and Oatman (1971), Odebiyi and Oatman (1972), Verma and Bindra (1974), Sathe (1984a, 1984b), Tagwa (1984), Sathe and Bhoje (1998), Sathe and Margaj (2001), Zenil *et al.* (2004) etc., attempted host parasitoid density relationships in Braconid (Parasitoid) and Lepidoptera (Host) models. Whereas, Leong and Oatman (1968), Nikam and Basarkar (1981), Sathe and Nikam (1985), Sathe (1990), Sathe and Shanthakumar (1989), Wang and Kellar (2002), Wang *et al.* (2004) etc., attempted host parasitoid density relationship in Ichneumonid parasitoids.

Materials and Methods

A. bosei

Laboratory culture of parasitoids and hosts were used in the experiments. 6-7 day old *A. moorei* larvae were exposed in densities 5, 10, 20, 30 and 50 to mated females of *A. moorei* for 24 hours in oviposition cage 25cm×25cm×25cm (L×W×H). After exposure the host larvae were reared into perforated plastic containers for further development and adult emergence. The parasitoids were fed with 50 per cent honey and hosts with leaves of sorghum crop. The experiment was replicated 5 times and conducted at 25±2°C, 65±5 per cent R.H., 12 hr photoperiod.

G. spodopterae

Optimum host density for *G. spodopterae* was determined by exposing 3-4 day old caterpillars of *S. litura* in densities of 5, 10, 20, 30, 40 and 50 to the mated females for 24 h in a rearing cage (25×25×25 cm). After 24 h the caterpillars of *S. litura* were separated into perforated plastic containers for further development of parasitoid emergence or adult moth emergence or unknown host mortality. The caterpillars of *S. litura* were fed with soybean leaves, whereas the parasitoids were fed with 50 per cent honey solution. The experiment was conducted at 25±2°C, 60±5 per cent R.H., and 12 hr (L : D) photoperiod and replicated 5 times for confirming the results.

X. pedator

In order to determine the optimum host density for *X. pedator* 1-2 days old *C. partellus* pupae were exposed in densities of 5, 10, 20, 30 and 40 to mated females of *X. pedator*. The exposure was in oviposition cage (25×25×25 cm) for 24 h. The exposed pupae were placed in petri dishes for further observations for parasitoid emergence and/or number of adult moths and host mortality. The pupae were kept in separate container. Parasitoids were fed with 50 per cent honey solution. The entire experiment was conducted under laboratory conditions (25±2°C, 65±5% R.H., and 12 hr photoperiod). The experiment was replicated 5 times to confirm the results.

Results

A. bosei

The results recorded in Table 5.1 and Fig. 5.1 showed that the number of parasitoid obtained from host density 30 was highest, compared to those produced from other host densities 5, 10, 30 and 50. The mean percentage of parasitism was also highest (50.00%) at 30 host density and 5, 10, 20 and 50 showed 20.00, 40.00, 42.00 and 30.00 mean percentage of parasitism respectively.

G. spodopterae

The results tabulated in Table 5.2 and Fig. 5.2 showed that the maximum progeny production was obtained when parasitoid exposed to the density of 20 hosts with parasitism of 43.00 per cent. However, the minimum was noticed on 5 host density with parasitism of 22.00 per cent. The per cent of parasitism varied with host density of 10, 30, 40 and 50 with parasitism percentage of 34.00, 39.00, 36.00 and 24.00 respectively.

X. pedator

The results showed in Table 5.3 and Fig. 5.3 indicated that the *X. pedator* cause 39.00 per cent parasitism at host density of 30 on *C. partellus* caterpillars. Whereas, with host density 5 parasitoid showed lowest parasitism (23.00%). The mean per cent parasitization varies from 28.00, 33.33 and 30.40 per cent with host densities of 10, 20 and 40 respectively.

Table 5.1: Effect of host density on parasitism by *A. bosei*

Host Density	Number of Hosts Exposed	Unknown Percent Mortality (Mean±SE)	Percent Moth Emergence (Mean±SE)	Percent Mean Parasitism (Mean±SE)
5	25	20.00±0.55	60.00±0.88	20.00±0.66
10	50	30.00±0.88	30.00±0.75	40.00±0.48
20	100	15.00±1.25	43.00±0.39	42.00±1.10)
30	150	15.00±0.65	35.00±1.25	50.00±0.82
50	250	20.00±1.10	50.00±0.82	30.00±1.25

Table 5.2: Effect of host density on parasitism by *G. spodopterae*

Host Density	Number of Hosts Exposed	Unknown Percent Mortality (Mean±SE)	Percent Moth Emergence (Mean±SE)	Percent Mean Parasitism (Mean±SE)
5	25	33.80±0.34	44.20±0.55	22.00±0.89
10	50	31.00±0.45	35.00±0.89	34.00±0.55
20	100	13.00±0.84	44.00±1.45	43.00±0.89
30	150	25.50±0.38	35.50±0.84	39.00±0.84
40	200	22.00±0.84	42.00±1.10	36.00±1.45
50	250	24.60±0.45	51.40±0.38	24.00±0.84

Table 5.3: Effect of host density on parasitism by *X. pedator*

Host Density	Number of Hosts Exposed	Unknown Percent Mortality (Mean±SE)	Percent Moth Emergence (Mean±SE)	Percent Mean Parasitism (Mean±SE)
5	25	19.00±0.45	58.00±0.84	23.00±0.55
10	50	12.00±0.84	60.00±1.00	28.00±0.84
20	75	10.67±0.55	56.00±0.89	33.33±0.71
30	100	12.00±0.89	49.00±1.10	39.00±0.84
40	125	11.20±1.48	58.40±2.30	30.40±1.14

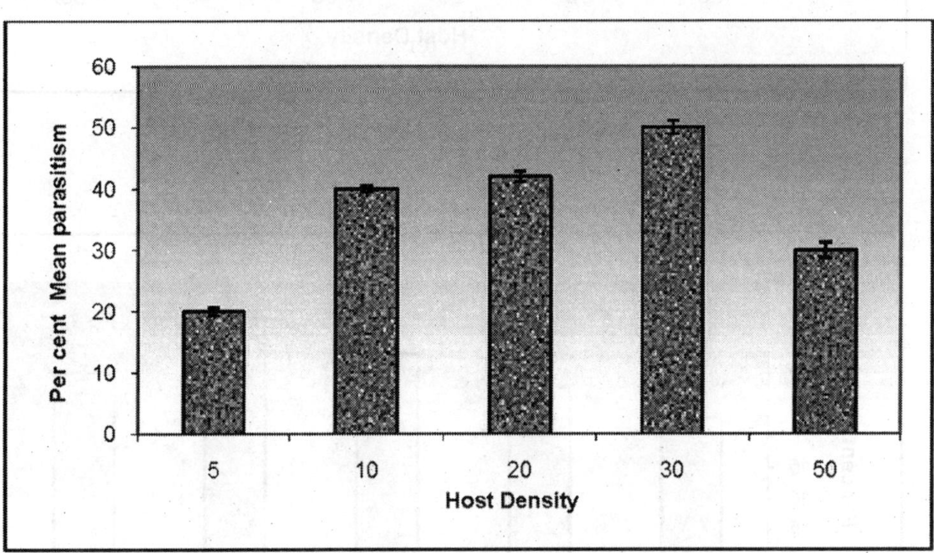

Fig. 5.1: **Host density relationship in *A. bosei***

Discussion

Cardona and Oatman (1971) reported 90 host density of *Keiferia lycopersicella* (Walsingham) as optimum density for maximum parasitism by *A. dignus*. They also reported that the percentage of parasitization increased with the increase in number of hosts (30, 60 and 90) per replicate but a decrease in parasitization occurred in all replicates when 120 larvae were offered. In *Apanteles obliquae* beyond host density 50, the percentage parasitism was reduced while, it was in increasing order from densities 5 to 50 (Sathe and Bhoje, 1998). In present study decrease in per cent parasitism was found after 40 host density suggesting the appropriate exposure of the larvae.

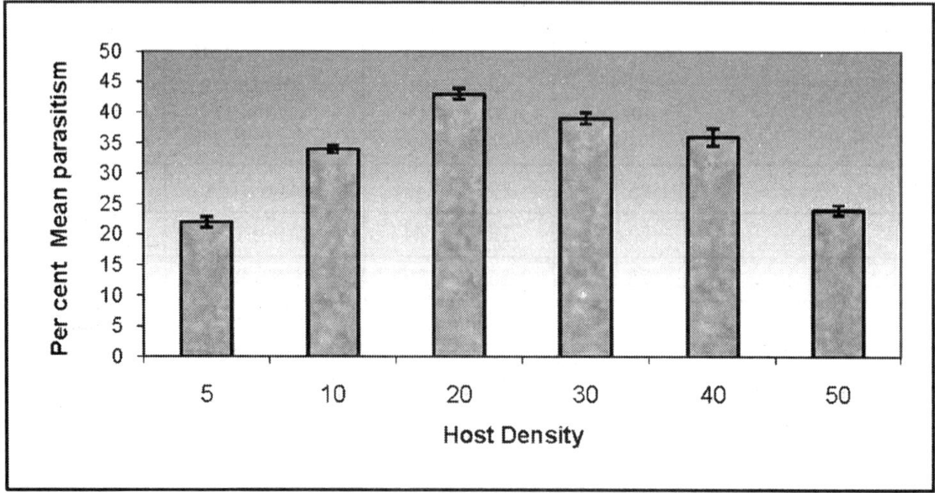

Fig. 5.2: **Host density relationship in *G. spodopterae***

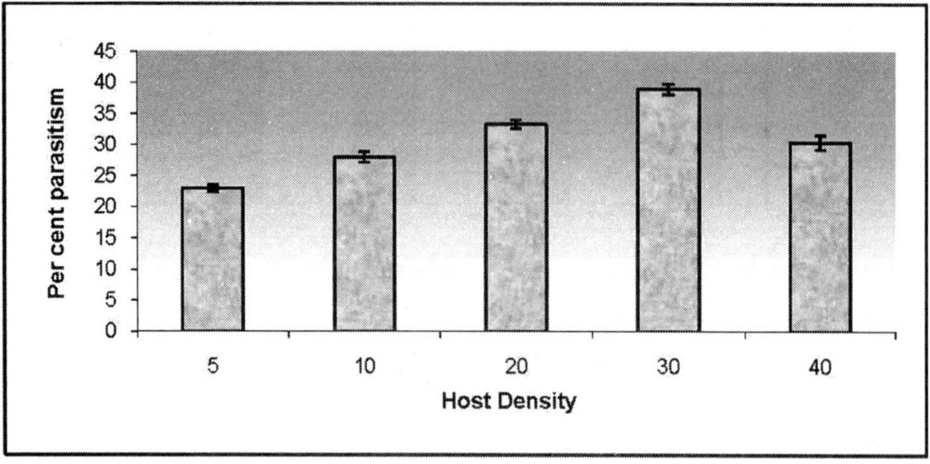

Fig. 5.3: **Host density relationship in *X. pedator***

The host density dependent factor for parasitism was studied in *Orgilus lepidus* Muesebeck, a primary parasitoid of potato tuber moth, *P. operculella* by Oatman *et al.* (1969) by providing a single potato tuber infected with 50, 100 and 150 hosts larvae and tubers with divided host larvae. They observed that the oviposition by *O. lepidus* generally did not increase when hosts were divided between additional tubers. The optimum host density was 150 hosts for maximum progeny production.

Sathe (1984b) studied the host density influence and reproductive potential of *Cotesia diurnii* R. and N., larval parasitoid of *Exelastis atomosa* Wals. He reported that parasitoids obtained from host density 40 were highest in number. Host densities 10, 20, 30 and 50 showed 16.12, 17.85, 18.44 and 16.33 per cent parasitism respectively. Sathe and Nikam (1985) studied influence of host density on percentage parasitism by *Diadegma trichoptilus* (Cameron), a larval parasitoid of *E. atomosa* and reported that the highest number of parasitoids obtained when 30 larvae were exposed for oviposition. At this density, the maximum parasitism was 21.66 per cent while at 10, 20, 40 and 50 densities the percentage of parasitism was 12.50, 17.50, 15.93 and 12.50 respectively. Sathe and Bhoje (1998) studied host density relationship in a parasitoid *A. obliquae* and a polyphagus pest *Spilosoma obliqua* (Walker). They reported that the host density 50 was the optimum for maximum parasitism on which yielded 54.00 per cent progeny production and the host densities 5, 10, 20, 30 and 100 have produced 30, 34, 42, 46 and 48 per cent progeny production respectively. In the present study of *A. bosei*, the optimum host density for maximum progeny production was 30 and the mean highest percentage of parasitism was 50.

In *C. haywardi*, an ichneumonid parasitoid of *P. operculella* the optimum host density was 75 larvae per tuber for maximum progeny production (Leong and Oatman, 1968). The observations indicated that there was great variation between replicates at the same larval densities and they further observed that mean emergence at higher densities was from 3 per cent to 15 per cent less than at 75 host density.

According to Nikam and Basarkar (1981) *C. chlorideae*, an internal larval parasitoid of *H. armigera* executed maximum parasitization with host density 40. Similarly, Sathe (1990) reported 50 host density as optimum for maximum parasitization (62%) by *Diadegma argenteopilosa* Cameron (Hymenoptera: Ichneumonidae), a larval parasitoid of *S. litura*.

Very recently, Sathe and Bhosale (2011) conducted host density relationship of *Diadegma insulare* (Cameron) against *P. xylostella* and reported that, the optimum host density for maximum progeny production was 100 and the mean highest percentage of parasitism was 38.50 per cent.

HOST AGE SELECTION

INTRODUCTION

The host age selection is a complex phenomenon. However it has extreme importance in introduction, colonization and mass production of parasitoids in biological pest control. The shape, size, movement, sound, immunological stability and age of host plays very crucial role (Vinson 1972, Sathe 2014). In parasitoids, the parasitization may be affected by the age and stage (egg, larva, pupa, adult) of the host in which female lay the eggs (Rabinovich, 1970; Nechols and Kikuchi, 1985). The quality of the environment affects the development and fitness offspring produced (Trimble and Wellington, 1979; van Alphen and Janssen, 1982; Pierce and Elgar, 1985). Therefore, desirable attribute of the environment is the availability of quantity and quality food resources. Thus, the habitat of biocontrol agent also plays an important role in biological pest control (Sathe, 2014).

Older hosts may provide less nutrition for offspring feeding and hence for their development (King, 1990), but in gregarious parasitoids older hosts with sufficient larger size are preferred as a part of sufficient food for the larvae. Therefore, comparing with young hosts, parasitization was more likely to be unsuccessful in older hosts (King, 1994).

Parasitization experience in older hosts with young hosts may affect future offspring production. Many time oviposition on older hosts may increases stress on the ovipositor for drilling and diminishes energy available for successive progeny production.

The review of literature indicates that, Nobel and Graham (1966), Lingren *et al.* (1970), Lewis (1970), Oatman and Platner (1974), Schmidt (1975), Smilowitz and Iwantsch (1975), Thurston and Postley (1978), Sathe and Ingawale (1993), Sathe and Jadhav (2001), Sathe (2014, 2015) etc., have made significant contribution on study of host age selection in parasitic hymenoptera.

Materials and Methods

A. bosei

The caterpillars of *A. moorei* with 30 host densities were exposed in a glass cage of size 25×25×30cm to mated females of *A. bosei*. After 24 hr of exposure the caterpillars were removed and placed in separate container for recording the parasitoid emergence. The hosts were fed with the leaves of sorghum and the parasitoids with 50 per cent honey solution. The experiment was replicated 5 times for confirming the results.

G. spodopterae

S. litura caterpillars with the density of 30 were placed with mated females of *G. spodopterae* in glass cage (25×25×30cm, size). 1 day old to 13 day old *S. litura* larvae were exposed to parasitoid for 24 hours for detecting preference of host age by the parasitoid. Parasitized larvae were separated in another container for further development and parasitoid emergence. The caterpillars of *S. litura* were reared on soybean plant. Each experiment was replicated 5 times for confirming the results.

X. pedator

The optimum host age for maximum parasitization were analyzed by exposing *C. partellus* pupae of age ranging from 1 day old to 10 day old the mated female of *X. pedator* in glass cage of size 25×25×30cm and kept for 24 hr. After oviposition the pupae were transferred in petri plates at 25±2°C, 60±5 per cent R.H., and 12 hr photoperiod for adult emergence of parasitoids. Daily records were maintained for the emergence of adult parasitoids. Percentage of host mortality (pupae from which neither parasitoid nor moth emerged), percentage of adult moth emergence and percentage of hosts from which parasitoid emerged have been analyzed for determining optimum host age for getting maximum progeny production of parasitoids and from which number of parasitoid progenies (male : female) were recorded. The parasitoids were fed with 50 per cent honey, which enhances the longevity ratio of female with longer lifespan of adults.

Results

A. bosei

Results on the host age selection by *A. bosei* are tabulated in Table 5.4 and Fig. 5.4. The results indicated that the maximum parasitization was recorded in the caterpillars of 6 days old with 34.00 per cent parasitism. The parasitoid showed a stable response towards the host stage in between 5 to 8 day old larvae with parasitism of 18.00, 34.00, 28.00 and 18.00 respectively. The per cent parasitism was descended towards both ends from the fourth day.

G. spodopterae

The results showed in Table 5.5 and Fig. 5.5 stated that the parasitoid preferred first two instars of *S. litura* to oviposit their eggs. *G. spodopterae* showed extreme parasitism with the host age of 4 days (38.00% parasitism), while from that the parasitism should be slower down towards both ends. Both 3 days and 5 days old hosts showed 34.00 per cent parasitism and 2 days and 6 days old hosts showed 32.00 and 30.00 per cent parasitism respectively. Hence, it can be assumed that for mass production of *G. spodopterae* the hosts exposed for parasitism must be within first two instars for acquiring maximum progeny production.

X. pedator

The results on host age selection by *X. pedator* are represented in Table 5.6 and Fig. 5.6. The parasitoid caused maximum parasitism towards 2 days old pupae of *C. partellus* with 38.00 per cent parasitism. The parasitoid showed a very good result when host age ranges between 1 day old to 4 day old pupae and moderate results for 5 to 7 day old pupae of lepidopteran stem borer. Whereas, beyond 9 days there was no parasitism noticed by *X. pedator*.

Table 5.4: Host age selection of *A. bosei*

Host Age in Days	Total No. of Hosts Tried	No. of Parasitoids Produced			Percent Mortality (Mean±SE)	Percent Moth Emergence (Mean±SE)	Percent Mean Parasitism (Mean±SE)
		Male	Female	Total			
1.	50	00	00	00	11.00±1.14	89.00±0.84	00
2.	50	00	00	00	14.00±1.14	86.00±0.84	00
3.	50	03	01	04	10.00±1.00	82.00±0.84	08.00±0.84
4.	50	03	03	06	16.00±1.14	72.00±0.84	12.00±0.84
5.	50	04	05	09	10.00±1.00	72.00±1.48	18.00±1.30
6.	50	08	09	17	06.00±0.89	60.00±0.71	34.00±1.14
7.	50	09	05	14	06.00±0.55	66.00±2.07	28.00±1.92
8.	50	03	06	09	10.00±1.00	78.00±0.84	18.00±1.30
9.	50	00	04	04	10.00±1.00	72.00±0.84	08.00±0.84
10.	50	00	00	00	08.00±0.84	92.00±0.84	00
11.	50	00	00	00	06.00±0.89	94.00±0.89	00

Table 5.5: Host age selection of *G. spodopterae*

Host Age in Days	Total No. of Hosts Tried	No. of Parasitoid Produced			Percent Mortality (Mean±SE)	Percent Moth Emergence (Mean±SE)	Percent Mean Parasitism (Mean±SE)
		Male	Female	Total			
1.	50	06	04	10	16.00±1.14	64.00±1.14	20.00±0.82
2.	50	07	09	16	16.00±1.34	52.00±1.79	32.00±0.97
3.	50	08	09	17	16.00±1.14	50.00±1.22	34.00±0.95
4.	50	08	11	19	14.00±0.89	48.00±0.84	38.00±1.20
5.	50	09	08	17	12.00±1.10	54.00±1.52	34.00±0.95
6.	50	06	09	15	16.00±0.89	54.00±1.67	30.00±0.85
7.	50	07	07	14	20.00±1.41	52.00±1.48	28.00±0.84
8.	50	05	06	11	14.00±0.89	64.00±1.14	22.00±0.88
9.	50	03	05	08	14.00±1.34	70.00±2.00	16.00±0.63
10.	50	02	03	05	18.00±1.30	72.00±0.84	10.00±0.71
11.	50	01	02	03	12.00±0.84	82.00±1.48	06.00±0.67
12.	50	00	00	00	12.00±1.30	88.00±1.30	00
13.	50	00	00	00	10.00±1.00	90.00±1.00	00

Table 5.6: Host age selection of *X. pedator*

Host Age in Days	Total No. of Hosts Tried	No. of Parasitoid Produced			Percent Mortality (Mean±SE)	Percent Moth Emergence (Mean±SE)	Percent Mean Parasitism (Mean±SE)
		Male	Female	Total			
1.	50	06	08	14	06.00±0.45	66.00±3.11	28.00±1.62
2.	50	08	11	19	03.00±0.55	60.00±1.22	38.00±1.16
3.	50	08	07	15	06.00±1.30	64.00±2.77	30.00±1.05
4.	50	06	05	11	06.00±1.10	71.00±1.79	22.00±1.16
5.	50	04	06	10	05.00±0.71	74.00±2.39	20.00±1.10
6.	50	04	04	08	01.00±0.45	82.00±1.14	16.00±1.16
7.	50	02	03	05	25.00±1.87	65.00±2.24	10.00±0.82
8.	50	02	02	04	05.00±0.71	86.00±0.84	08.00±0.74
9.	50	00	00	00	28.00±2.30	72.00±2.30	00
10.	50	00	00	00	16.00±1.30	84.00±1.30	00

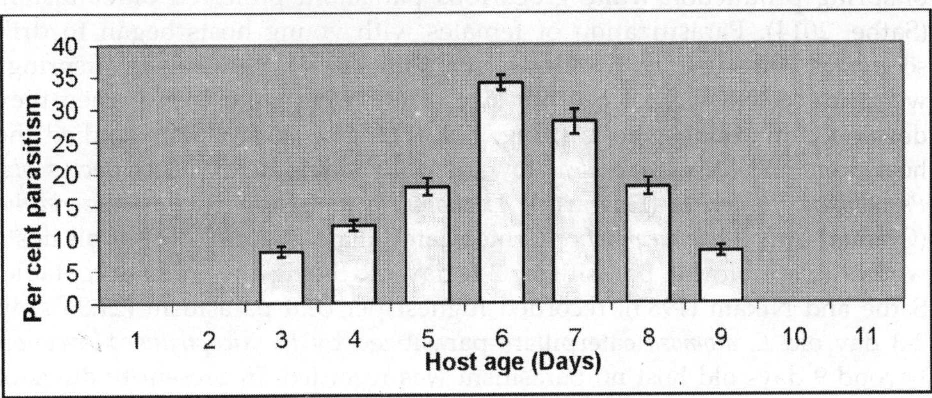

Fig. 5.4: **Host age selection of *A. bosei***

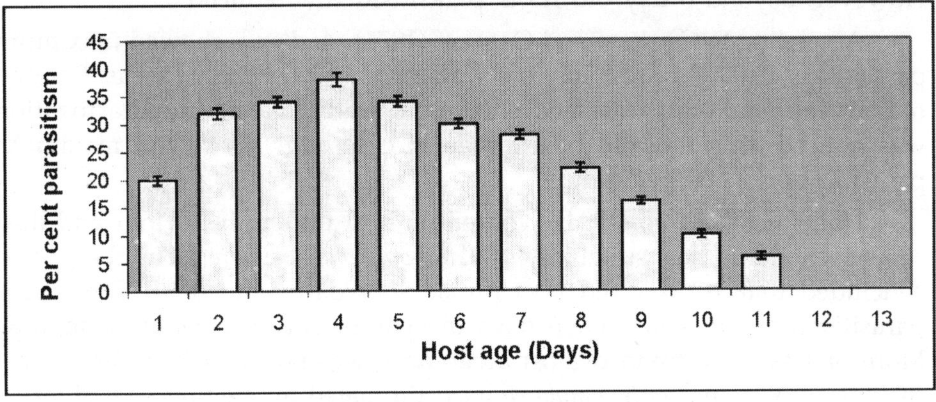

Fig. 5.5: **Host age selection of *G. spodopterae***

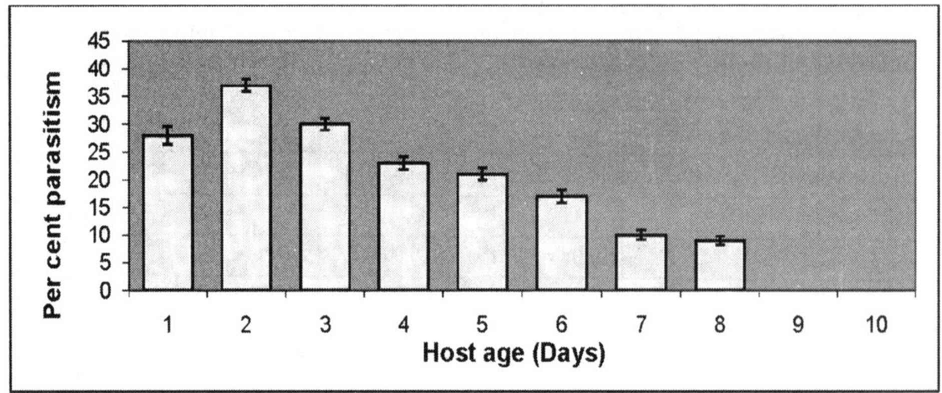

Fig. 5.6: **Host age selection of *X. pedator***

Discussion

Female of solitary parasitoids preferred young instars for more offspring production while gregarious parasitoid preferred older instars (Sathe, 2014). Parasitization of females with young hosts began to drill sooner as compared with older hosts (King, 1994). Survival of offsprings were unaffected by host age but size of offspring were larger when they developed in younger hosts (King, 1990). Lingren *et al.* (1970), studied the host preference of *C. chlorideae* towards four lepidopteran host species *viz; Pseudoletia unipuncta* (Hawarth), *Trichopulsia ni* (Hubner), *Prodenia ridinia* (Cramer) and *Prodenia praefica* Grote. Caterpillars (1-8 day old) of all hosts were succeptible for parasitism, 2-6 day old being the most acceptable. Sathe and Nikam (1985), recorded highest per cent parasitism (21.33%) in 2-3 day old *E. atomosa* caterpillars parasitized by *D. tricoptellus*. However, beyond 9 days old host no parasitism was recorded. In present findings of *X. pedator* the maximum parasitism was noticed on 2 days old pupae. However, beyond 6 day old hosts parasitism was reduced.

According to Cardona and Oatman (1971), *A. dignus* showed maximum parasitism (48.00%) on 2-3 day old *K. lycopersicella* larvae whereas, 8-9 day old larvae remain unparasitized. In present study, maximum parasitization was noticed on 6 day old host larvae in case of *A. bosei* with maximum parasitization 34.00 per cent.

Hailemichael *et al.* (1994), worked on host finding behaviour and host age selection and host suitability of *Xanthopimpla stemmator* (Thunberg) and concluded that 1-5 day old host pupae showed averaged 31-37 per cent parasitism, whereas beyond 6 days the parasitism declines at rapid rate. More or less same trend of host acceptance was noted in *X. pedator*. Host seeking activity in *Xanthopimpla sp* was stimulated by the presence of larval frass, host odour and movement of host species. In the present experiment, 6 day old host of *A. moorei* showed highest per cent parasitism of 37.00 per cent. Above and below the host age of 6 days the parasitism declines continuously. Results suggested that the present parasitoids are good candidates for biological control of lepidopteran pests in agroecosystem.

HOST SPECIFICITY

INTRODUCTION

The laboratory culture of parasitoids and their hosts including alternate hosts are essential for their mass culture as a very crucial part of biological pest control programme. The large scale production of parasitoids on alternate hosts can strengthen the biocontrol progamme on commercial level. The parasitoid minimizes the parasitism when lacks the appropriate host species, the said criteria restricted the in-vitro mass culture of parasitoids. Therefore, detection of host specificity in parasitoids has great importance in mass rearing of parasitoids. Parasitoids varied their attack in laboratory on different host species by preferring the appropriate host for parasitism (Salt, 1935a). Salt (1935b) and Vinson (1975) described the four sequential steps which help parasitoids for parasitism refer to habitat selection, host location, host acceptance and host suitability.

Habitat selection of parasitoids possesses the prime role in the host selection. Parasitoid grooms in the definite environment for the detection of host. Once parasitoid detected the proper habitat, they find suitable hosts afterwards. In host finding behaviour of parasitoid, chemicals released through the hosts play a very significant role (Vinson, 1972). Audio visual and chemical stimuli play an important role in host selection (Sathe 2014, 2015). Review of literature indicates that Azuma and Kitano (1971), Lingren and Nobel (1972), Jackson *et al.* (1979), Hooper and King (1984), Somchoudhary and Dutt (1988), Sathe and Santhakumar (1992) and Sathe (2014) etc., have worked on host specificity in parasitic hymenoptera.

Materials and Methods

To investigate the host specificity of parasitoids *A. bosei*, *G. spodopterae* and *X. pedator* the various host species were exposed at appropriate host age and density. The laboratory reared hosts and parasitoids were utilized for present investigations. Mated females of *A. bosei* were exposed to *A. moorei*, *Thiocidas postica* Wlk, *Udaspes folus* (Cramer), *S. obliqua*, *H. armigera* with mixed host density of 50. *G. spodopterae* females were exposed to *H. armigera*, *S. litura*, *Spodoptera exigua* (Hubner) whereas, females of *X. pedator* were exposed to *C. partellus*, *S. derogata*, *Bombyx mori* (Linn.), *Antheraea mylitta* Drury and *Actias selene* (Hubner) in a glass cage 25×25×30cm for 24 hour, afterwards separated in glass troughs and kept under observations of parasitoid or moth emergence. During experiment the parasitoids were fed with 50 per cent honey solution and the hosts were fed with there proper host plant parts. The experiment was conducted under laboratory conditions (25±2°C, 60±5% R.H., 12 hr photoperiod) and replicated 5 times for confirming the results.

Results

A. bosei

The host specificity of *A. bosei* is tabulated in Table 5.7 and Fig. 5.7. The result indicates the *A. moorei* was most preferred with maximum parasitization 41.00 per cent. The parasitoid showed following preference towards the host *T. postica* > *S. obliqua* > *U. folus* with parasitism of 37.00, 23.50 and 16.50 respectively, whereas caterpillars of *H. armigera* were not preferred by *A. bosei*.

G. spodopterae

The results represented in Table 5.8 and Fig. 5.8 indicated that the parasitoid gave most preference to *S. litura* (38.00 %). The order of preference given by parasitoids was *H. armigera* > *S. exigua* > *M. separata* with parasitism of 32.00, 27.00 and 08.00 respectively.

X. pedator

The results recorded in Table 5.8 and Fig. 5.8 showed that *B. mori* was the most preferred host for maximum parasitization (42.00%) while *A. selene* recorded minimum parasitization (15.00%). The order of host specificity given by *X. pedator* was *B. mori* > *A. mylitta* > *C. partellus* > *S. derogata* > *A. selene*. *A. mylitta* showed 34.00 per cent parasitism and the agricultural pests like: *C. partellus* and *S. derogata* showed 25.00 and 21.00 per cent parasitism respectively.

Table 5.7: Host preference of *A. bosei*

Host Species	Host Density	Percent Host Mortality (Mean±SE)	Percent Moth Emergence (Mean±SE)	Percent Mean Parasitism (Mean±SE)
A. moorei	50	04.00±0.85	55.00±0.57	41.00±1.35
T. postica	50	02.00±0.85	61.00±0.64	37.00±0.75
S. oblique	50	07.50±2.54	69.00±0.83	23.50±1.10
U. folus	50	09.00±1.24	74.50±0.75	16.50±0.55
H. armigera	50	15.00±1.10	85.00±0.68	00.00±0.00

Table 5.8: Host preference of *G. spodopterae*

Host Species	Host Density	Percent Host Mortality (Mean±SE)	Percent Moth Emergence (Mean±SE)	Percent Mean Parasitism (Mean±SE)
S. litura	50	16.00±0.85	46.00±0.68	38.00±0.45
H. armigera	50	05.00±1.25	63.00±0.55	32.00±1.10
S. exigua	50	07.00±0.78	66.00±1.00	27.00±0.75
M. seperata	50	03.00±0.55	89.00±0.45	08.00±0.57

Table 5.9: Host preference of *X. pedator*

Host Species	Host Density	Percent Host Mortality (Mean±SE)	Percent Moth Emergence (Mean±SE)	Percent Mean Parasitism (Mean±SE)
B. mori	50	35.00±3.08	23.00±6.00	42.00±4.69
A. mylitta	50	52.00±3.39	14.00±5.83	34.00±2.55
A. selene	50	54.60±4.39	30.40±4.34	15.00±4.18
C. partellus	50	12.00±2.35	63.00±6.24	25.00±5.43
S. derogate	50	15.40±1.82	63.60±5.03	21.00±3.67

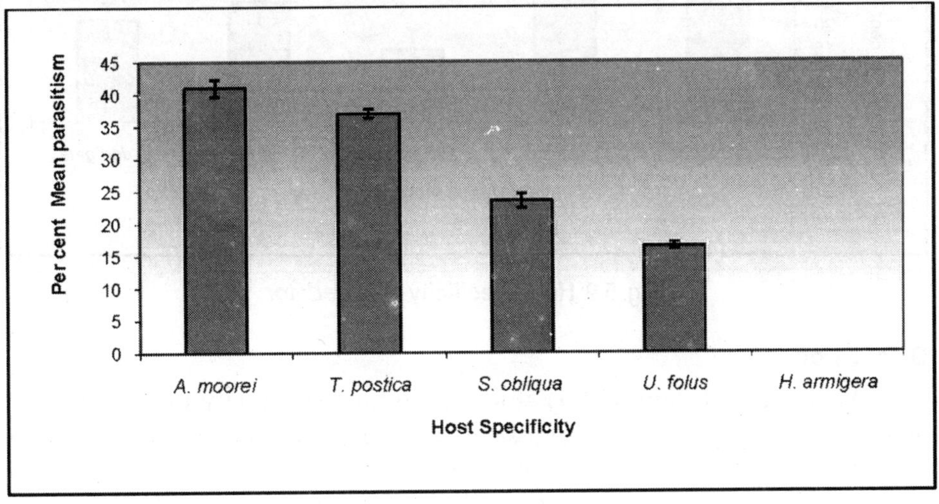

Fig. 5.7: **Host specificity of *A. bosei***

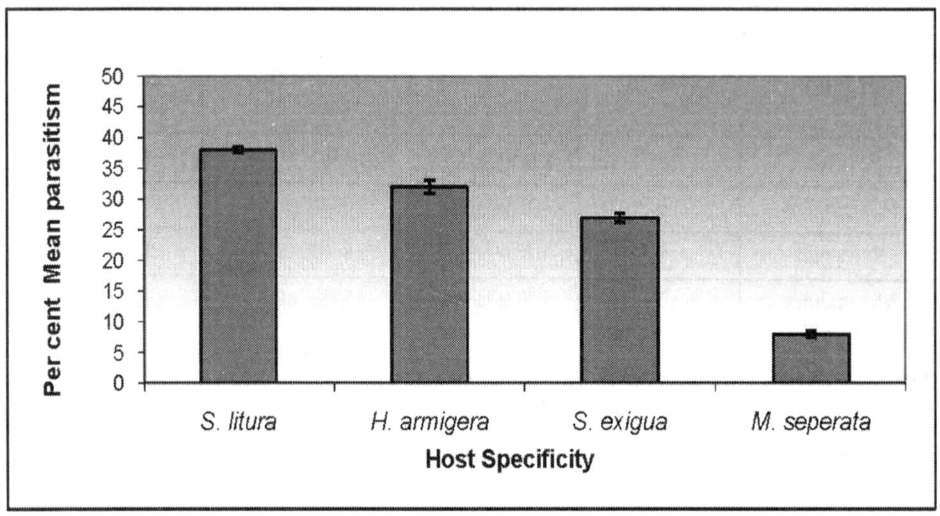

Fig. 5.8: **Host specificity of *G. spodopterae***

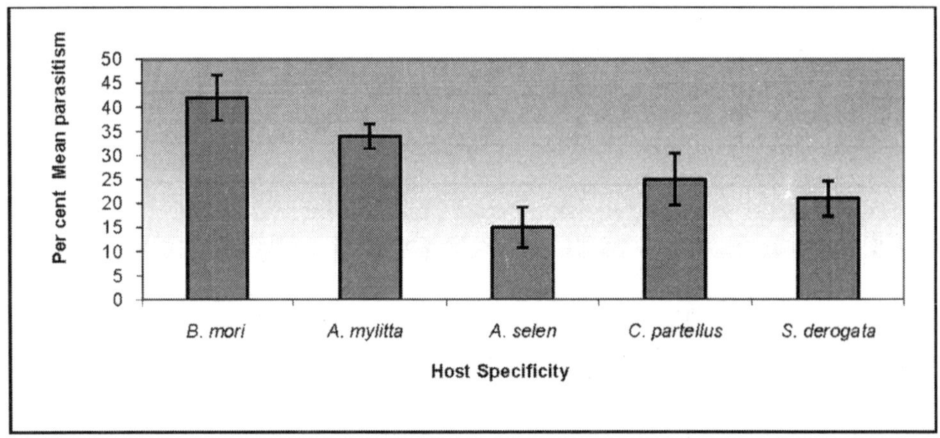

Fig. 5.9: **Host specificity of *X. pedator***

Discussion

Azuma and Kitano (1971) studied the host specificity of *C. glomeratus* against the caterpillars of *P. brassicae*, *Cydia pomonella* Druch and *P. rapae*. The order of preference was *P. brassicae* > *P. rapac* > *C. pomonella*. Similarly, Lingren and Nobel (1972) studied the host specificity in *Campoletis perdistinctus* Viereck against lepidopteran caterpillars of bollworms *Heliothis zea* (Hubn.), Tobacco budworm *Heliothis virescens* (F.), fall armyworm *Spodoptera frugiperda*, beet armyworm *S. exigua*, southern armyworm *Prodenia eridania* (Cramer), yellow stripped armyworm *Prodenia ornithogalli* Guenee, cabbage looper *Trichopulsia ni* (Hubner) and stated that the bollworms *H. zea*, Tobacco budworms *H. virescens* and fall armyworms *Spodoptera frugiperda* (Smith) are most preferred host by the parasitoid in the laboratory tests and cabbage looper *T. ni* was least preferred and caterpillars of beet armyworms were rejected.

Host preference of *C. blackburnii* (Hymenoptera: Braconidae) was studied by Jackson *et al.* (1979), towards cotton bollworm *H. zea*, pink bollworm *Pectinophora gossypiella*, beet armyworm *S. exigua*, cabbage looper *T. ni*, tobacco budworm *H. virescens* and saltmarsh caterpillar *Exstigmene acrea* (Drum.) and found that the parasitoid showed maximum preference to pink bollworms *P. gossypiella*. The order of preference was *T. ni* > *H. zea* > *H. virescens* > *S. exigua* whereas, parasitoid refused to saltmarsh caterpillar *E. acrea*.

Hooper and King (1984) observed the host preference in *Microbracon croceipes* Westmead and concluded that the caterpillars of *H. zea* and *H. virescens* were appropriate for efficient parasitization by parasitoid. They also reported the host age and density dependent factor for getting the maximum progeny production. In the present study 50 host densities of mixed hosts, *A. moorei*, *T. postica*, *S. obliqua* and *U. folus* have been tried and the most preferred host was *A. moorei*. Somchoudhary and Dutt (1988) reported the host specificity of parasitoids *Trichogramma perkinsi* and *Trichogramma australicum* and found that out of seven field pests studied, *E. atomosa* were most preferred host for both parasitoids. Parasitoids showed higher parasitization, shortening of lifespan and maximized the adult longevity with longer oviposition period on *E. atomosa* eggs. Besides that, they also reported the host preference of these two parasitoids on *C. partellus* and *H. armigera* and studied the above aspects and found the preference of *T. perkinsi* was more towards the eggs of *H. armigera* and the eggs of *C. partellus* were preferred by *T. australicum*. Similarly, they also studied the host preference against the eggs of *A. janata* but the least parasitization was noticed. They concluded that the parasitization varied according to the hosts exposed for oviposition. The size of egg for the egg parasitoid played a very crucial role in parasitism, as the size of egg was large the total number of eggs laid by the parasitoids was comparable to observed in case of *E. atomosa*, *C. partellus* and *H. armigera*.

Sathe and Santhakumar (1992) studied the host preference in *C. chlorideae* towards the caterpillars of *H. armigera*, *S. litura*, *S. exigua* and *E. atomosa*. The order of preference shown by parasitoid was *H. armigera* > *S. litura* > *S. exigua*. whereas, the caterpillars of *E. atomosa* were totally refused for parasitization. The present study will be helpful for providing basic knowledge of hosts preference needed for designing biocontrol programmes of agricultural insect pests.

Field Efficacy of Parasitoids

INTRODUCTION

Field efficacy of biocontrol agent plays a prime importance in the success of biocontrol programme. A better knowledge of the parasitoid behaviour is useful in timing and enumerating field releases of parasitoids (Battisti, 1989). Potential of any biocontrol agent is dependent on their rapid establishment in the field and their work against the pest population. Application of broad spectrum insecticides interfere the population of biocontrol agents hence, there is a need to synthesize the compatible pesticides for biocontrol agents and their rapid use for the management of agricultural pests. Multiple species of natural enemies commonly attack single host species (Price 1971, Hawkins 1990, Polis 1991, Hawkins and Mills 1996, Polis and Strong 1996). However, most of the experiments on parasitism have only focused on inspection of single parasitoid species at a time (Sih *et al.* 1998). Therefore, attempt has been made to investigate the types of parasitoids and their field efficacy with respect to parasitism in various pest insects. Review of literature indicates that Sathe *et al.* (1986), Sathe (1987), Battisti (1989), Ellers *et al.* (1998), Gerling *et al.* (2001), Bogran *et al.* (2002), Sathe and Chougule (2006), Abd-Rabou (2011), Ahmad *et al.* (2012) and Sathe and Chougule (2014) etc., worked on field efficacy of hymenopterous parasitoids.

Materials and Methods

Field efficacy of selected parasitoids was studied from 2010-13 from the study area of different tehsils of districts Kolhapur, Sangli and Satara. The field efficacy was analyzed by the concept of naturally occurring field efficacy of parasitoids. The host insects of *A. bosei*, *G. spodopterae* and *X. pedator* have been collected from different study spots of Western Maharashtra. The collected hosts (pests) were reared on their respective host plants in the laboratory for parasitoid emergence. The parasitoids were identified by consulting appropriate literatures. The per cent of parasitism was calculated by counting larvae parasitized out of 100 individuals. Records were also made on unknown mortalities in the host insects and the per cent moth emerged during the rearing of field collected hosts. The study spots selected are noted in tables 19-44.

Results

A. bosei

The average per cent field efficacy of *A. bosei* for the year 2010-13 noted in Table 6.1 to 6.9 and Fig. 6.7 to 6.15 from Kolhapur, Sangli and Satara region. For the year 2010-11, average per cent field efficacy for Kolhapur, Sangli and Satara was 20.93, 15.86 and 18.67 respectively. For year 2011-12 it ranged from 23.27, 19.80 and 22.47 respectively. Similarly for the year 2012-13 average field efficacy of Kolhapur 29.13 per cent, Sangli 23.67 per cent and Satara 23.53 per cent was observed.

G. spodopterae

The average per cent field efficacy of *G. spodopterae* from Kolhapur, Sangli and Satara region for the year 2010-11 was 19.00, 21.47 and 18.13 respectively (Table 6.10 to 6.12 and Fig. 6.16 to 6.18). However, Table 6.13 to 6.15 and Fig. 6.19 to 6.21 represents the average per cent field efficacy from Kolhapur, Sangli and Satara region (30.26, 24.53 and 25.13 respectively) for the year 2011-12. Similarly, for 2012-13 the average field efficacy 24.93, 21.47 and 24.40 from Kolhapur, Sangli and Satara respectively (Table 6.16 to 6.18 and Fig. 6.22 to 6.24).

X. pedator

For the year 2010-11 average per cent field efficacy of *X. pedator* were 19.27, 15.80 and 13.80 from Kolhapur, Sangli and Satara region respectively which was represented in Table 6.19 to 6.21, Fig. 6.25 to 6.27. The average per cent field efficacy during 2011-12 was 18.73, 16.60 and 13.74 from Kolhapur, Sangli and Satara region respectively (Table 6.22 to 6.24, Fig. 6.28 to 6.30). For 2012-13 average per cent field efficacy of above regions were 23.67, 25.67 and 25.47 respectively which was tabulated in Table 6.25 to 6.27 and Fig. 6.31 to 6.33.

During 2010 to 2013 maximum average field efficacy of *A. bosei* and *G. spodopterae* was found in Kolhapur region followed by Satara and Sangli. However, for *X. pedator* pattern of maximum average field efficacy was noticed with Kolhapur > Sangli > Satara.

Plate - 1 (Figs. 1-6) **Agriculture crop fields.** Fig. 6.1: **Jowar variety: M 35-1,** Fig. 6.2: **Paddy variety: Sonam,** Fig. 6.3: **Wheat variety: Lok-1,** Fig. 6.4: **Gram variety: Vijay,** Fig. 6.5: **Soyabean variety: JS-335,** Fig. 6.6: **Ber variety: Local**

Table 6.1: Field efficacy of *A. bosei* from Kolhapur region (2010-11)

Sr. No.	Name of Tehsil	Percent Parasitism (Mean±SE)	Percent Host Mortality (Mean±SE)	Percent Moth Emergence (Mean±SE)
1.	Kagal	19.67±8.74	5.33±2.52	75.00±10.00
2.	Radhanagari	19.67±4.04	3.33±1.53	77.00±3.61
3.	Panhala	24.00±3.61	4.33±3.51	71.67±4.04
4.	Shahuwadi	21.33±1.15	4.51±1.53	74.33±2.08
5.	Hatkanagale	20.00±4.58	6.33±2.31	73.67±4.73
	Average	20.93±4.42	4.73±2.28	74.33±4.89

Table 6.2: Field efficacy of *A. bosei* from Sangli region (2010-11)

Sr. No.	Name of Tehsil	Percent Parasitism (Mean±SE)	Percent Host Mortality (Mean±SE)	Percent Moth Emergence (Mean±SE)
1.	Miraj	12.67±2.08	5.00±3.46	82.33±5.51
2.	Shirala	15.33±4.04	6.00±2.00	78.67±5.13
3.	Walwa	17.33±4.51	4.67±3.06	78.00±1.73
4.	Palus	16.33±5.51	6.33±2.52	77.33±7.57
5.	Tasgaon	17.66±0.58	5.33±6.34	77.00±3.14
	Average	15.86±3.34	5.47±3.48	78.67±4.62

Table 6.3: Field efficacy of *A. bosei* from Satara region (2010-11)

Sr. No.	Name of Tehsil	Percent Parasitism (Mean±SE)	Percent Host Mortality (Mean±SE)	Percent Moth Emergence (Mean±SE)
1.	Patan	20.33±8.96	6.33±1.53	73.33±7.57
2.	Wai	15.67±5.69	2.67±2.45	81.67±5.77
3.	Lonand	19.33±5.69	6.00±4.36	74.67±6.66
4.	Karad	19.33±4.51	5.33±3.51	75.33±5.48
5.	Koregaon	18.67±3.21	4.67±1.53	76.67±2.08
	Average	18.67±5.61	5.00±2.49	76.33±5.75

Table 6.4: Field efficacy of *A. bosei* from Kolhapur region (2011-12)

Sr. No.	Name of Tehsil	Percent Parasitism (Mean±SE)	Percent Host Mortality (Mean±SE)	Percent Moth Emergence (Mean±SE)
1.	Kagal	25.33±2.31	6.00±3.61	68.67±5.86
2.	Radhanagari	26.00±3.61	4.33±2.08	69.67±2.08
3.	Panhala	24.33±4.16	3.67±0.58)	72.00±3.61
4.	Shahuwadi	25.00±3.61	5.67±4.16	69.33±5.51
5.	Hatkanagale	15.67±2.52	6.33±1.53	78.00±3.61
	Average	23.27±3.24	5.20±2.39	71.53±4.13

Table 6.5: Field efficacy of *A. bosei* from Sangli region (2011-12)

Sr. No.	Name of Tehsil	Percent Parasitism (Mean±SE)	Percent Host Mortality (Mean±SE)	Percent Moth Emergence (Mean±SE)
1.	Miraj	20.00±6.24	3.33±1.53	76.67±6.35
2.	Shirala	19.00±7.21	5.33±2.52	75.67±6.03
3.	Walwa	20.67±6.11	4.33±3.51	75.00±8.19
4.	Palus	20.00±2.65	6.00±3.00	74.00±3.61
5.	Tasgaon	19.33±6.81	6.67±2.52	74.00±4.36
	Average	19.80±4.33	5.13±2.71	71.53±4.79

Table 6.6: Field efficacy of *A. bosei* from Satara region (2011-12)

Sr. No.	Name of Tehsil	Percent Parasitism (Mean±SE)	Percent Host Mortality (Mean±SE)	Percent Moth Emergence (Mean±SE)
1.	Patan	20.67±6.43	4.33±1.53	75.00±7.94
2.	Wai	19.00±5.00	5.00±4.00	76.00±1.00
3.	Lonand	24.67±6.43	3.00±1.00	72.33±5.51
4.	Karad	25.00±5.57	4.67±3.06	70.33±8.14
5.	Koregaon	23.00±8.67	3.66±1.73	73.33±4.43
	Average	22.47±5.80	4.13±2.53	73.40±6.15

Table 6.7: Field efficacy of *A. bosei* from Kolhapur region (2012-13)

Sr. No.	Name of Tehsil	Percent Parasitism (Mean±SE)	Percent Host Mortality (Mean±SE)	Percent Moth Emergence (Mean±SE)
1.	Kagal	28.33±3.06	6.33±1.53	65.33±4.04
2.	Radhanagari	26.67±9.50	2.67±1.53	70.67±10.60
3.	Panhala	29.00±6.24	6.00±4.36	65.00±6.08
4.	Shahuwadi	30.00±1.00	5.33±3.51	64.67±4.04
5.	Hatkanagale	31.67±8.08	4.67±1.53	63.67±8.50
	Average	29.13±5.58	5.00±2.49	65.87±6.65

Table 6.8: Field efficacy of *A. bosei* from Sangli region (2012-13)

Sr. No.	Name of Tehsil	Percent Parasitism (Mean±SE)	Percent Host Mortality (Mean±SE)	Percent Moth Emergence (Mean±SE)
1.	Miraj	25.67±0.58	5.33±2.52	69.00±3.00
2.	Shirala	23.33±9.02	3.33±1.53	73.33±10.50
3.	Walwa	22.67±1.53	4.33±3.51	73.00±2.00
4.	Palus	18.67±3.21	6.33±2.52	75.00±5.57
5.	Tasgaon	27.00±6.00	6.33±2.31	66.67±8.08
	Average	23.47±4.07	5.13±2.48	71.40±5.83

Table 6.9: Field efficacy of *A. bosei* from Satara region (2012-13)

Sr. No.	Name of Tehsil	Percent Parasitism (Mean±SE)	Percent Host Mortality (Mean±SE)	Percent Moth Emergence (Mean±SE)
1.	Patan	23.67±7.02	4.00±3.61	72.33±5.51
2.	Wai	20.67±6.81	4.00±3.46	75.33±9.50
3.	Lonand	25.67±6.03	3.33±2.52	71.00±5.29
4.	Karad	22.33±3.79	3.00±1.73	74.67±3.51
5.	Koregaon	25.33±2.52	3.67±1.53	71.00±1.73
	Average	23.53±5.23	3.60±2.57	72.87±5.11

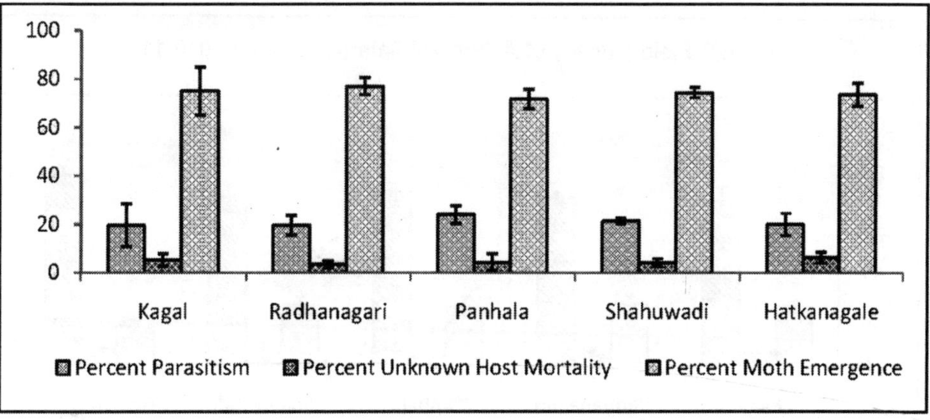

Fig. 6.7: **Field efficacy of *A. bosei* of Kolhapur region for 2010-11**

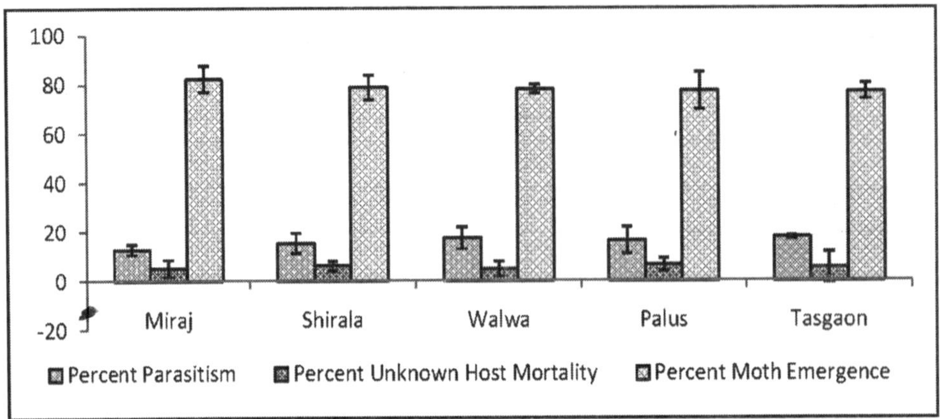

Fig. 6.8: **Field efficacy of *A. bosei* of Sangli region for 2010-11**

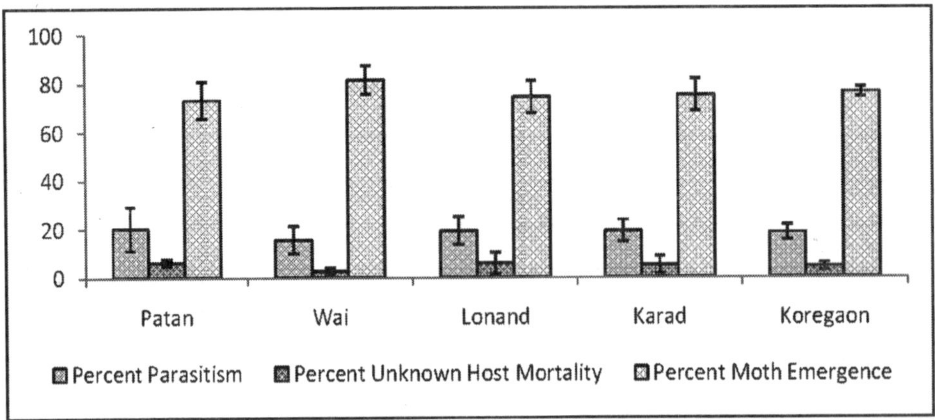

Fig. 6.9: **Field efficacy of *A. bosei* of Satara region for 2010-11**

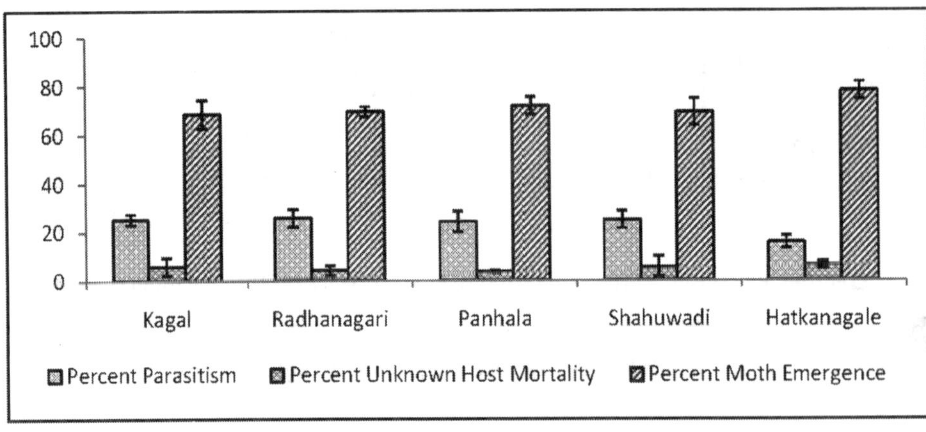

Fig. 6.10: **Field efficacy of *A. bosei* of Kolhapur region for 2011-12**

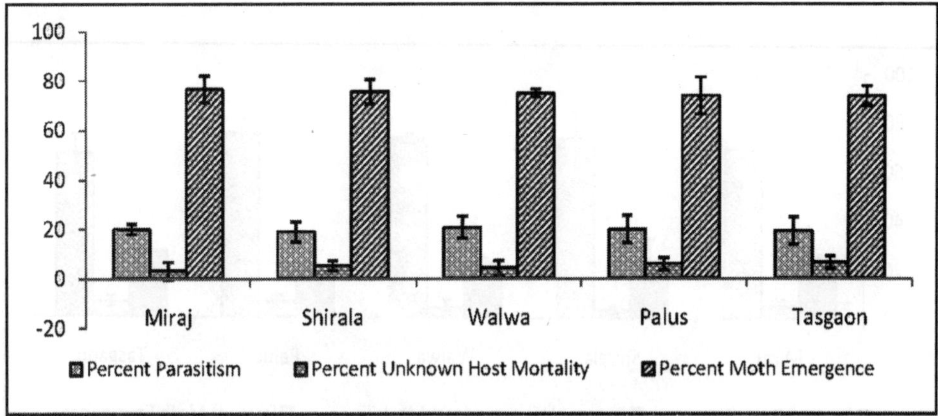

Fig. 6.11: **Field efficacy of *A. bosei* of Sangli region for 2011-12**

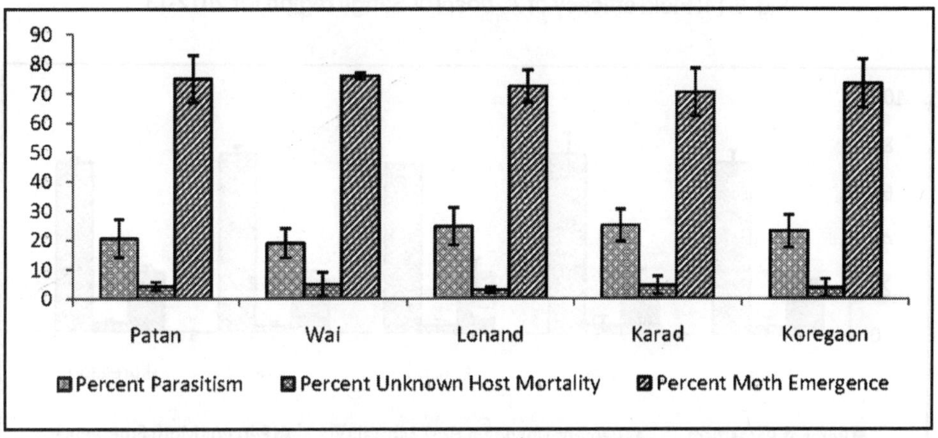

Fig. 6.12: **Field efficacy of *A. bosei* of Satara region for 2011-12**

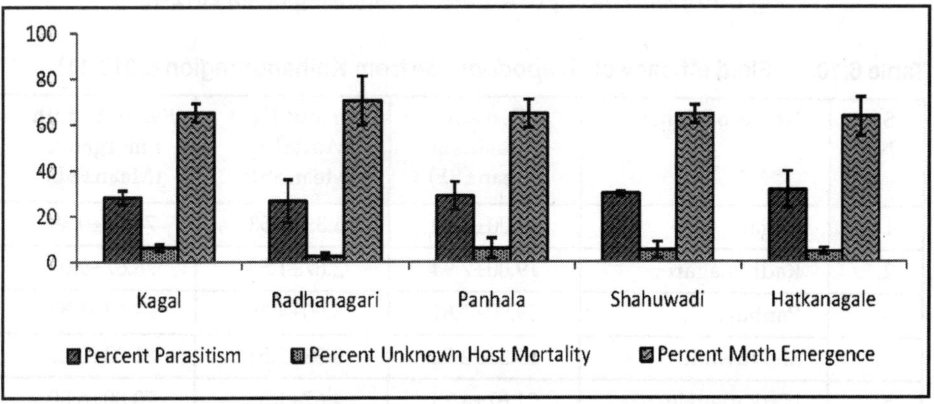

Fig. 6.13: **Field efficacy of *A. bosei* of Kolhapur region for 2012-13**

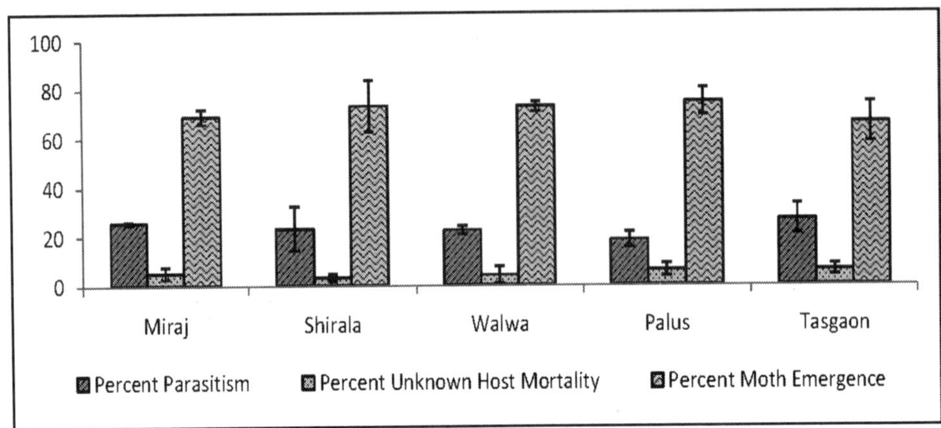

Fig. 6.14: **Field efficacy of *A. bosei* of Sangli region for 2012-13**

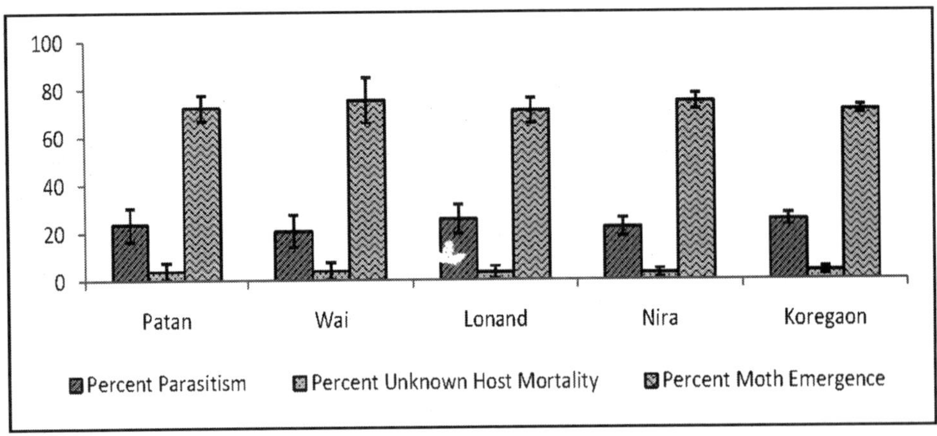

Fig. 6.15: **Field efficacy of *A. bosei* of Satara region for 2012-13**

Table 6.10: Field efficacy of *G. spodopterae* from Kolhapur region (2010-11)

Sr. No.	Name of Tehsil	Percent Parasitism (Mean±SE)	Percent Host Mortality (Mean±SE)	Percent Moth Emergence (Mean±SE)
1.	Kagal	20.00±3.00	6.33±1.53	74.33±0.58
2.	Radhanagari	19.00±7.94	2.67±1.53	76.67±9.02
3.	Panhala	19.00±3.61	6.00±4.36	77.33±1.53
4.	Shahuwadi	15.33±2.52	5.33±3.51	81.33±3.21
5.	Hatkanagale	21.67±4.73	4.67±1.53	73.00±6.00
	Average	19.00±4.36	5.00±2.49	76.53±4.07

Table 6.11: Field efficacy of *G. spodopterae* from Sangli region (2010-11)

Sr. No.	Name of Tehsil	Percent Parasitism (Mean±SE)	Percent Host Mortality (Mean±SE)	Percent Moth Emergence (Mean±SE)
1.	Miraj	21.00±5.57	5.67±2.52	73.33±7.23
2.	Shirala	23.33±3.79	4.33±3.51	72.33±5.69
3.	Walwa	20.67±2.52	6.33±4.62	73.00±7.00
4.	Palus	19.00±6.08	3.33±1.53	77.67±6.66
5.	Tasgaon	23.33±0.58	5.33±2.08	71.33±1.53
	Average	21.47±3.71	5.00±2.85	73.53±5.62

Table 6.12: Field efficacy of *G. spodopterae* from Satara region (2010-11)

Sr. No.	Name of Tehsil	Percent Parasitism (Mean±SE)	Percent Host Mortality (Mean±SE)	Percent Moth Emergence (Mean±SE)
1.	Patan	20.00±2.00	2.00±1.73	78.00±3.61
2.	Wai	18.00±2.65	3.00±1.00	79.00±2.65
3.	Lonand	12.33±3.21	4.33±1.53	83.33±4.62
4.	Karad	19.00±4.36	3.33±2.52	77.67±6.66
5.	Koregaon	21.33±1.53	2.67±2.08	76.00±3.46
	Average	18.13±2.75	3.07±1.77	78.80±4.20

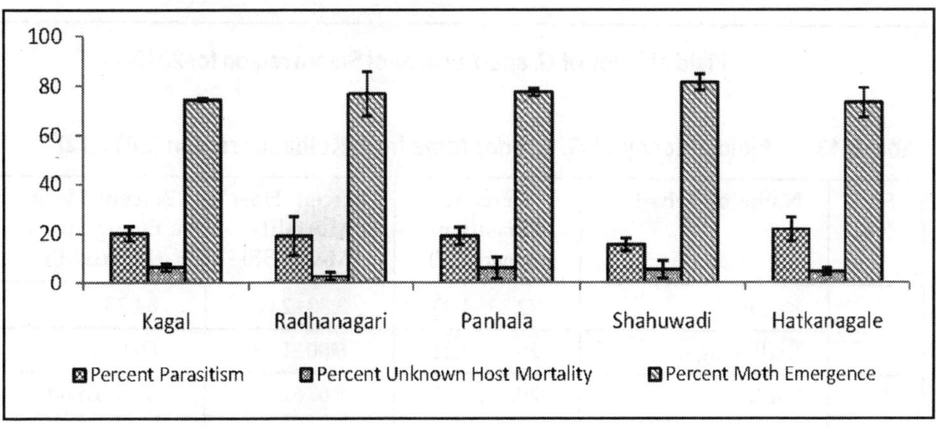

Field efficacy of *G. spodopterae* of Kolhapur region for 2010-11

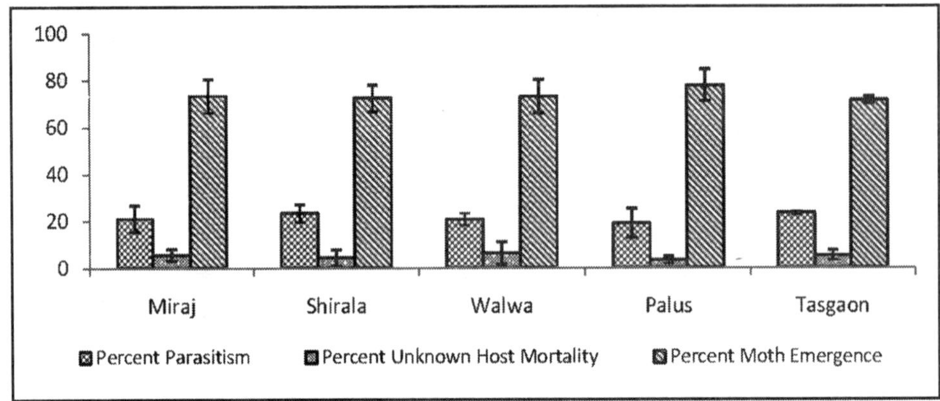

Field efficacy of *G. spodopterae* of Sangli region for 2010-11

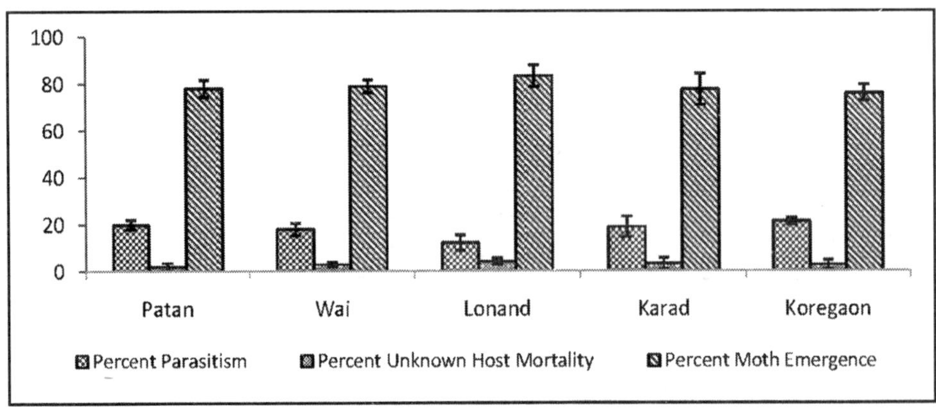

Field efficacy of *G. spodopterae* of Satara region for 2010-11

Table 6.13: Field efficacy of *G. spodopterae* from Kolhapur region (2011-12)

Sr. No.	Name of Tehsil	Percent Parasitism (Mean±SE)	Percent Host Mortality (Mean±SE)	Percent Moth Emergence (Mean±SE)
1.	Kagal	32.33±4.93	3.33±2.08	64.33±6.03
2.	Radhanagari	28.00±7.21	6.00±1.73	66.00±5.57
3.	Panhala	29.33±2.52	5.67±2.52	65.00±3.00
4.	Shahuwadi	32.33±10.26	4.33±1.53	63.33±11.68
5.	Hatkanagale	29.33±5.51	7.66±2.31	63.00±7.55
	Average	30.26±6.09	5.40±2.03	64.33±6.77

Table 6.14: Field efficacy of *G. spodopterae* from Sangli region (2011-12)

Sr. No.	Name of Tehsil	Percent Parasitism (Mean±SE)	Percent Host Mortality (Mean±SE)	Percent Moth Emergence (Mean±SE)
1.	Miraj	29.33±8.08	3.00±1.00	67.67±7.51
2.	Shirala	22.33±5.69	5.33±2.08	72.33±7.77
3.	Walwa	23.33±3.06	6.00±2.00	70.67±1.15
4.	Palus	19.67±1.53	5.66±2.89	74.67±3.51
5.	Tasgaon	28.00±3.61	4.00±1.73	68.00±5.29
	Average	24.53±4.39	4.80±1.94	70.67±5.05

Table 6.15: Field efficacy of *G. spodopterae* from Satara region (2011-12)

Sr. No.	Name of Tehsil	Percent Parasitism (Mean±SE)	Percent Host Mortality (Mean±SE)	Percent Moth Emergence (Mean±SE)
1.	Patan	30.33±8.14	3.67±2.08	66.00±9.85
2.	Wai	25.33±3.21	5.00±1.00	69.67±2.31
3.	Lonand	22.67±5.03	3.67±0.57	73.67±5.13
4.	Karad	24.00±7.21	5.67±3.06	70.33±7.57
5.	Koregaon	23.33±3.51	6.00±3.46	70.67±5.13
	Average	25.13±5.42	4.80±2.03	70.07±5.99

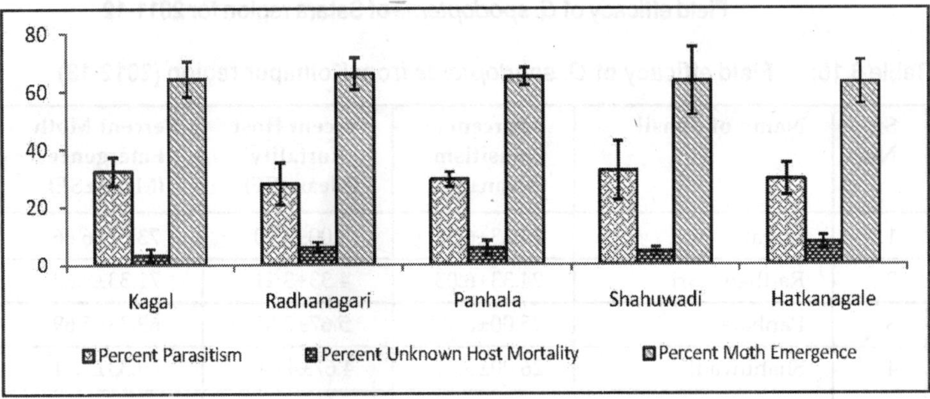

Field efficacy of *G. spodopterae* of Kolhapur region for 2011-12

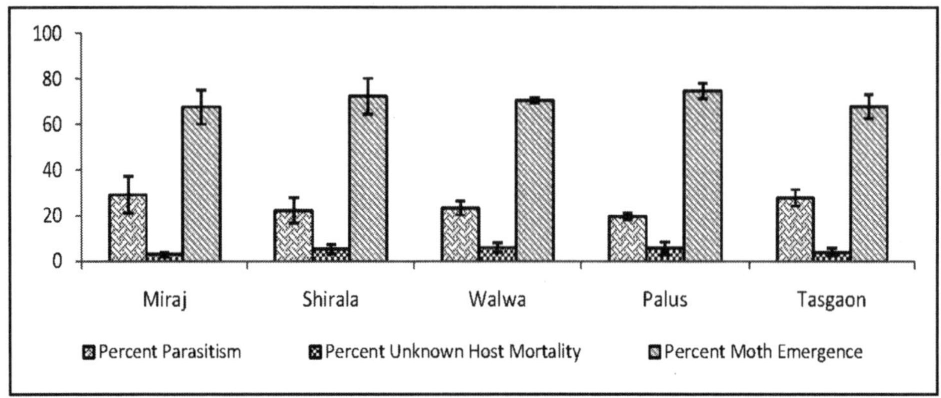

Field efficacy of *G. spodopterae* of Sangli region for 2011-12

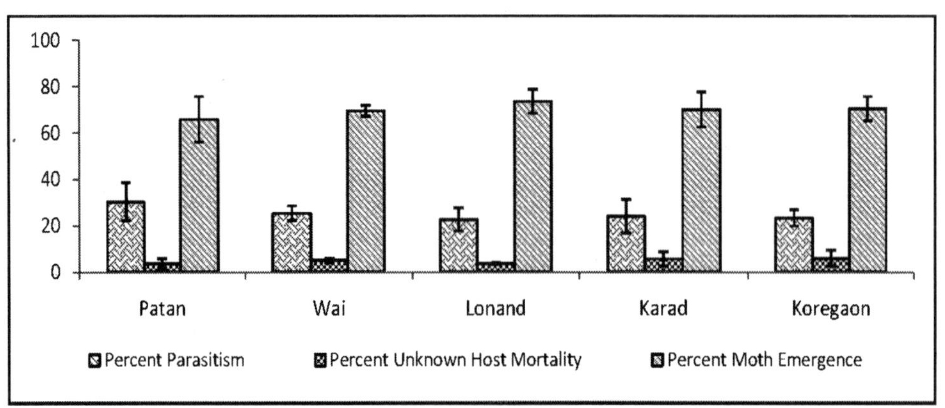

Field efficacy of *G. spodopterae* of Satara region for 2011-12

Table 6.16: Field efficacy of *G. spodopterae* from Kolhapur region (2012-13)

Sr. No.	Name of Tehsil	Percent Parasitism (Mean±SE)	Percent Host Mortality (Mean±SE)	Percent Moth Emergence (Mean±SE)
1.	Kagal	23.33±6.35	3.00±2.00	73.67±6.66
2.	Radhanagari	24.33±6.03	4.33±3.21	71.33±8.62
3.	Panhala	25.00±8.19	5.67±2.52	69.33±5.69
4.	Shahuwadi	26.00±3.61	4.67±4.04)	69.33±7.51
5.	Hatkanagale	26.00±4.36	3.67±1.53	70.33±2.89
	Average	24.93±5.71	4.27±2.66	70.80±6.27

Table 6.17: Field efficacy of *G. spodopterae* from Sangli region (2012-13)

Sr. No.	Name of Tehsil	Percent Parasitism (Mean±SE)	Percent Host Mortality (Mean±SE)	Percent Moth Emergence (Mean±SE)
1.	Miraj	21.00±5.57	5.67±2.52	73.33±7.23
2.	Shirala	23.33±3.79	4.33±3.51	72.33±5.69
3.	Walwa	20.67±2.52	6.33±4.62	73.00±7.00
4.	Palus	19.00±6.08	3.33±1.53	77.67±6.66
5.	Tasgaon	23.33±0.58	5.33±2.08	71.33±1.53
	Average	21.47±3.71	5.00±2.85	73.53±5.62

Table 6.18: Field efficacy of *G. spodopterae* from Satara region (2012-13)

Sr. No.	Name of Tehsil	Percent Parasitism (Mean±SE)	Percent Host Mortality (Mean±SE)	Percent Moth Emergence (Mean±SE)
1.	Patan	25.33±4.62	4.33±3.51	70.33±2.08
2.	Wai	22.33±9.45	4.00±3.46	73.67±9.02
3.	Lonand	23.33±6.43	3.33±2.52	73.33±4.51
4.	Karad	25.33±3.79	3.00±1.73	71.67 (±3.06
5.	Koregaon	25.67±2.52	3.33±1.53	74.00±1.00
	Average	24.40±5.36	3.60±2.55	72.60±3.93

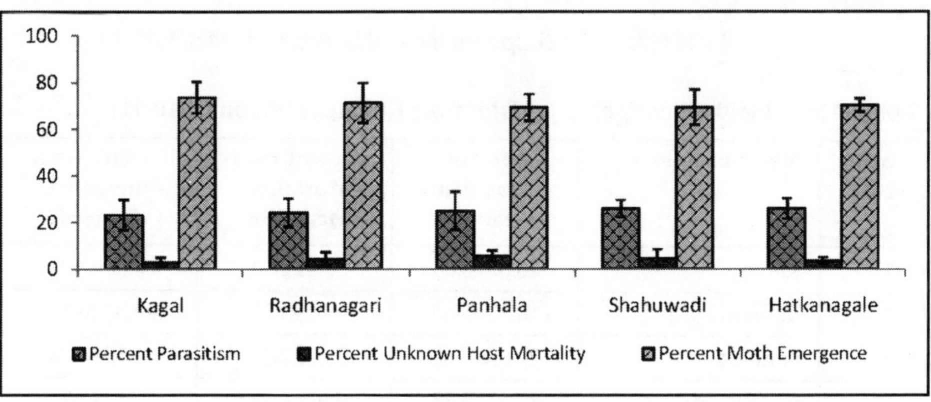

Field efficacy of *G. spodopterae* of Kolhapur region for 2012-13

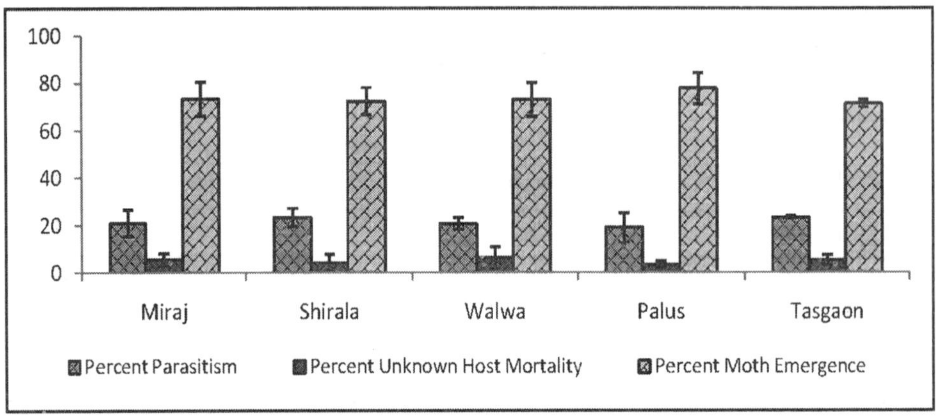

Field efficacy of *G. spodopterae* of Sangli region for 2012-13

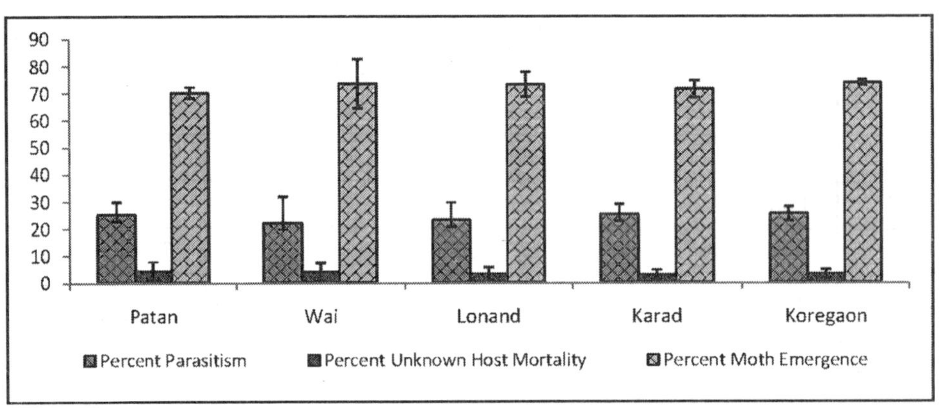

Field efficacy of *G. spodopterae* of Satara region for 2012-13

Table 6.19: Field efficacy of *X. pedator* from Kolhapur region (2010-11)

Sr. No.	Name of Tehsil	Percent Parasitism (Mean±SE)	Percent Host Mortality (Mean±SE)	Percent Moth Emergence (Mean±SE)
1.	Kagal	20.67±8.08	3.00±2.00	76.33±7.02
2.	Radhanagari	16.33±5.69	4.33±3.21	79.33±6.81
3.	Panhala	20.00±3.61	5.67±2.52	74.33±6.03
4.	Shahuwadi	17.67±4.73	4.67±4.04	77.67±3.79
5.	Hatkanagale	21.67±3.79	3.67±1.53	74.67±2.52
	Average	19.27±5.18	4.27±2.66	76.47±5.23

Table 6.20: Field efficacy of *X. pedator* from Sangli region (2010-11)

Sr. No.	Name of Tehsil	Percent Parasitism (Mean±SE)	Percent Host Mortality (Mean±SE)	Percent Moth Emergence (Mean±SE)
1.	Miraj	15.67±5.51	3.33±3.51	81.00±2.00
2.	Shirala	15.00±5.00	4.33±3.51	80.67±1.53
3.	Walwa	18.33±4.04	4.00±1.73	77.67±2.52
4.	Palus	15.33±2.52	4.66±2.52	80.00±2.00
5.	Tasgaon	14.67±4.16	5.00±4.58	80.33±7.37
	Average	15.80±4.25	4.27±3.17	79.93±3.08

Table 6.21: Field efficacy of *X. pedator* from Satara region (2010-11)

Sr. No.	Name of Tehsil	Percent Parasitism (Mean±SE)	Percent Host Mortality (Mean±SE)	Percent Moth Emergence (Mean±SE)
1.	Patan	13.33±4.16	3.33±1.53	83.33±3.79
2.	Wai	13.66±4.51	4.33±2.89	82.00±2.65
3.	Lonand	15.66±5.51	4.67±2.89	79.67±8.39
4.	Karad	12.33±2.52	5.00±2.00	82.67±2.08
5.	Koregaon	14.00±3.61	5.33±4.04	80.67±6.43
	Average	13.80±4.06	4.53±2.67	81.67±4.67

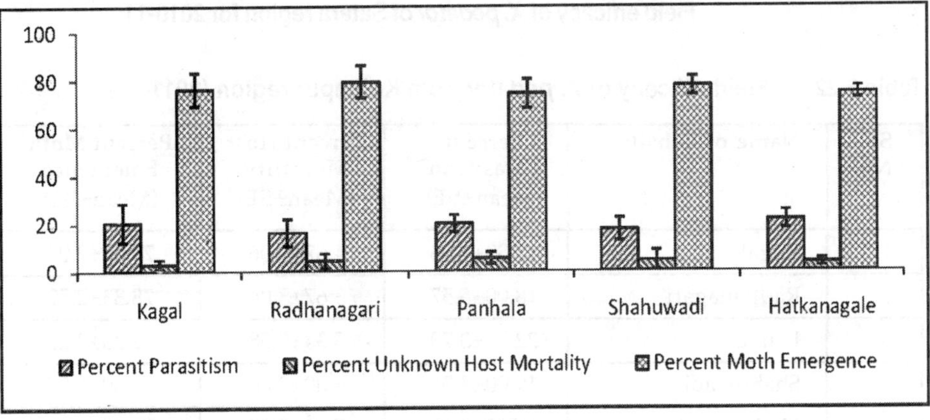

Field efficacy of *X. pedator* of Kolhapur region for 2010-11

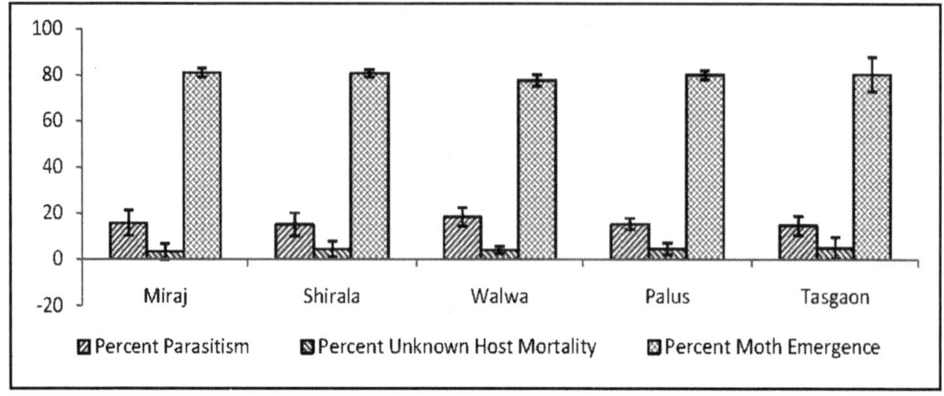

Field efficacy of *X. pedator* of Sangli region for 2010-11

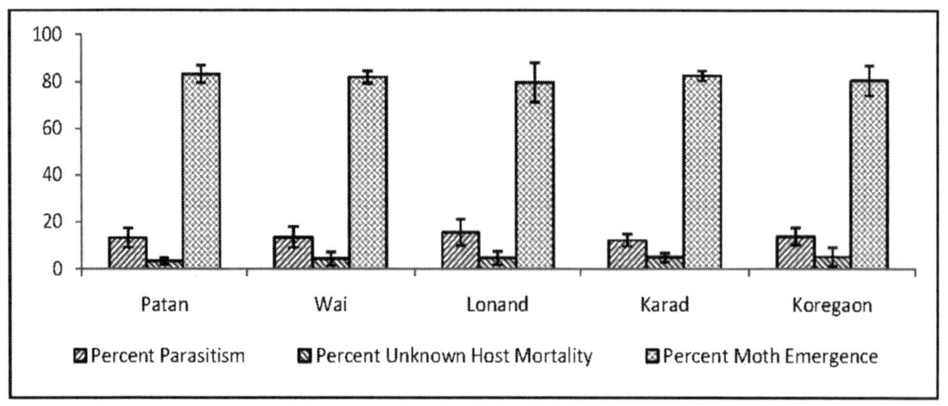

Field efficacy of *X. pedator* of Satara region for 2010-11

Table 6.22: Field efficacy of *X. pedator* from Kolhapur region (2011-12)

Sr. No.	Name of Tehsil	Percent Parasitism (Mean±SE)	Percent Host Mortality (Mean±SE)	Percent Moth Emergence (Mean±SE)
1.	Kagal	17.33±3.06	4.67±3.06	78.00±2.00
2.	Radhanagari	18.00±5.57	3.67±3.06	78.33±2.52
3.	Panhala	22.33±3.79	5.33±0.58	72.33±3.21
4.	Shahuwadi	19.00±4.36	6.00±3.00	75.00±5.57
5.	Hatkanagale	17.00±6.08	7.00±2.65	76.00±4.58
	Average	18.73±4.57	5.33±2.47	75.93±3.58

Table 6.23: Field efficacy of *X. pedator* from Sangli region (2011-12)

Sr. No.	Name of Tehsil	Percent Parasitism (Mean±SE)	Percent Host Mortality (Mean±SE)	Percent Moth Emergence (Mean±SE)
1.	Miraj	17.70±2.58	3.30±2.89	79.00±2.55
2.	Shirala	13.00±1.18	6.00±2.00	81.00±2.08
3.	Walwa	19.30±2.63	3.30±1.81	77.40±6.58
4.	Palus	16.70±3.77	3.30±1.53	80.00±4.48
5.	Tasgaon	16.30±5.51	4.00±3.00	79.70±7.55
	Average	16.60±4.25	3.99±3.17	79.42±3.08

Table 6.24: Field efficacy of *X. pedator* from Satara region (2011-12)

Sr. No.	Name of Tehsil	Percent Parasitism (Mean±SE)	Percent Host Mortality (Mean±SE)	Percent Moth Emergence (Mean±SE)
1.	Patan	12.70±3.43	3.00±4.18	84.30±1.88
2.	Wai	11.70±4.22	5.30±2.44	83.00±2.22
3.	Lonand	16.30±3.21	4.40±3.68	79.30±4.12
4.	Karad	13.70±1.92	4.70±5.24	81.60±1.88
5.	Koregaon	14.30±2.82	4.70±3.32	81.00±5.72
	Average	13.74±4.06	4.42±2.67	81.84±4.67

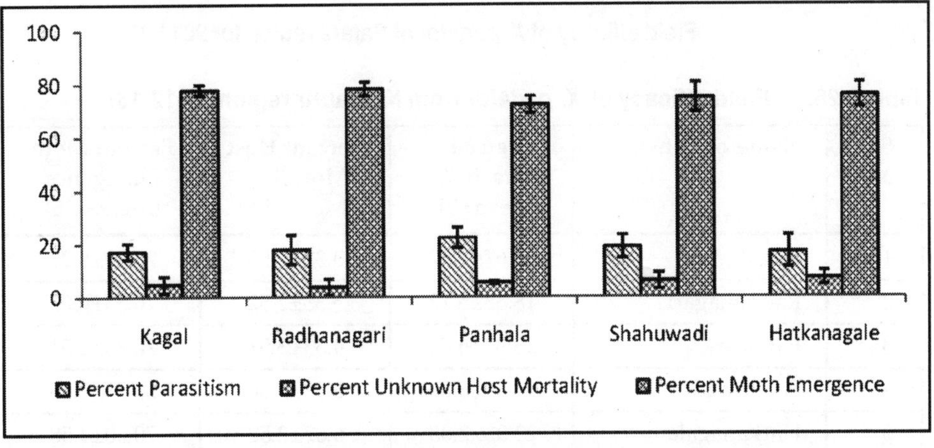

Field efficacy of *X. pedator* of Kolhapur region for 2011-12

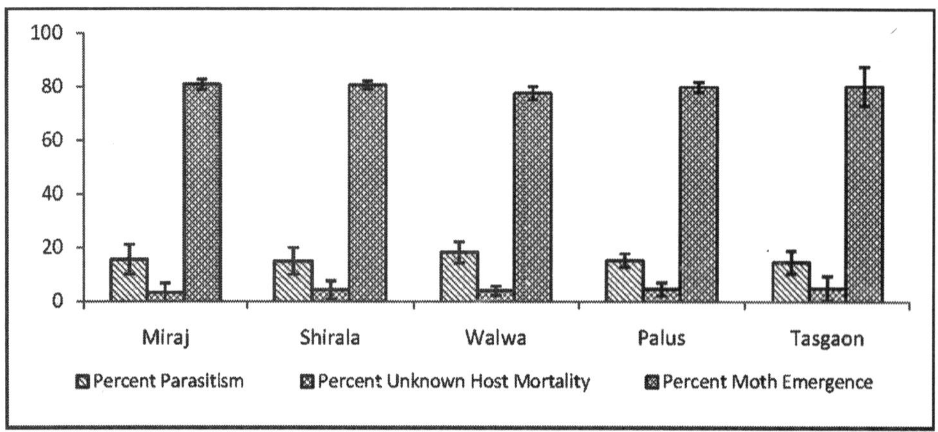

Field efficacy of *X. pedator* of Sangli region for 2011-12

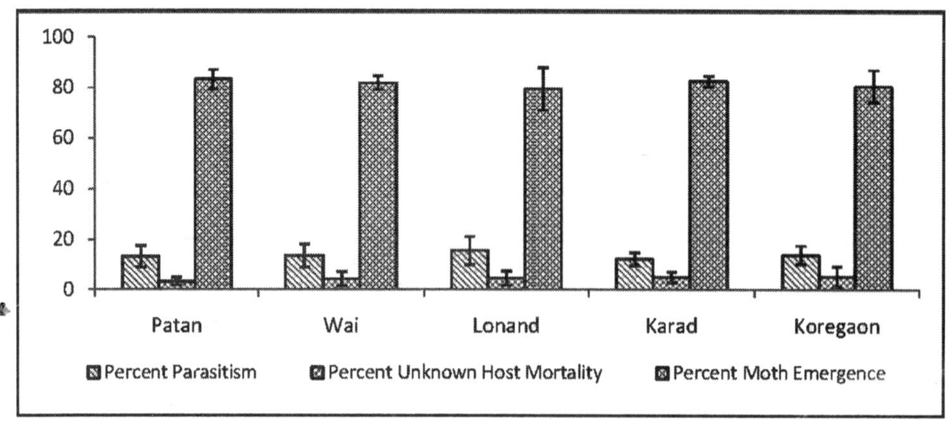

Field efficacy of *X. pedator* of Satara region for 2011-12

Table 6.25: Field efficacy of *X. pedator* from Kolhapur region (2012-13)

Sr. No.	Name of Tehsil	Percent Parasitism (Mean±SE)	Percent Host Mortality (Mean±SE)	Percent Moth Emergence (Mean±SE)
1.	Kagal	26.67±7.57	3.33±1.53	70.00±6.24
2.	Radhanagari	18.33±5.77	5.33±2.52	76.33±6.03
3.	Panhala	25.33±6.66	4.33±3.51	70.33±4.51
4.	Shahuwadi	24.67±6.66	6.00±3.00	69.33±9.45
5.	Hatkanagale	23.33±2.08	6.67±2.52	70.00±4.58
	Average	23.67±5.75	5.13±2.61	71.20±6.16

Table 6.26: Field efficacy of *X. pedator* from Sangli region (2012-13)

Sr. No.	Name of Tehsil	Percent Parasitism (Mean±SE)	Percent Host Mortality (Mean±SE)	Percent Moth Emergence (Mean±SE)
1.	Miraj	25.00±10.00	5.00±2.00	70.00±11.14
2.	Shirala	23.00±3.61	5.33±2.52	71.67±6.03
3.	Walwa	28.33±4.04	4.33±3.51	67.33±6.66
4.	Palus	25.67±2.08	6.00±3.00	68.33±4.04
5.	Tasgaon	26.33±4.73	6.00±2.65	67.67±6.43
	Average	25.67±4.89	5.33±2.73	69.00±6.86

Table 6.27: Field efficacy of *X. pedator* from Satara region (2012-13)

Sr. No.	Name of Tehsil	Percent Parasitism (Mean±SE)	Percent Host Mortality (Mean±SE)	Percent Moth Emergence (Mean±SE)
1.	Patan	26.00±10.54	5.33±2.52	68.67±13.01
2.	Wai	25.00±5.29	3.33±1.53	71.67±6.66
3.	Lonand	24.33±4.04	4.33±3.51	71.33±6.66
4.	Karad	24.00±2.65	4.33±1.53	71.67±2.52
5.	Koregaon	28.00±3.61	6.33±2.31	65.67±4.73
	Average	25.47±5.22	4.73±2.27	69.80±6.71

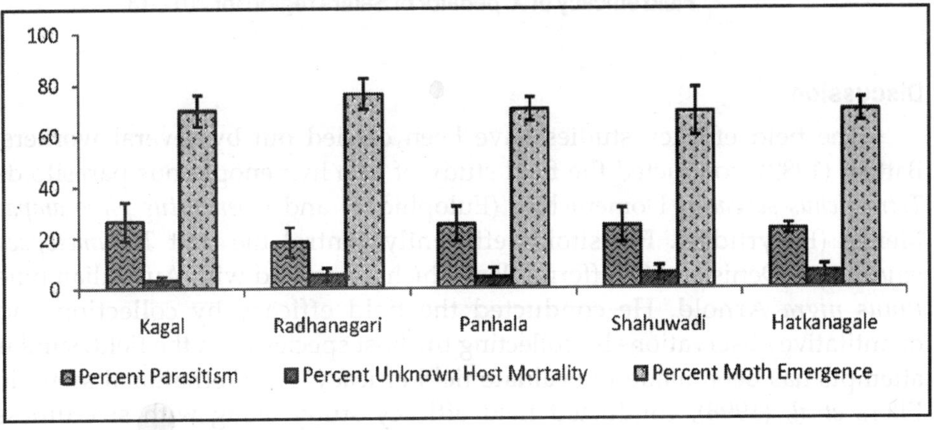

Field efficacy of *X. pedator* of Kolhapur region for 2012-13

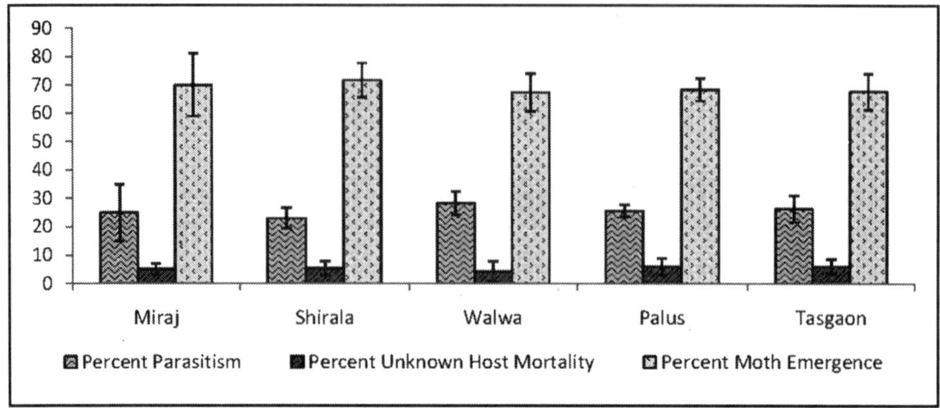

Field efficacy of *X. pedator* of Sangli region for 2012-13

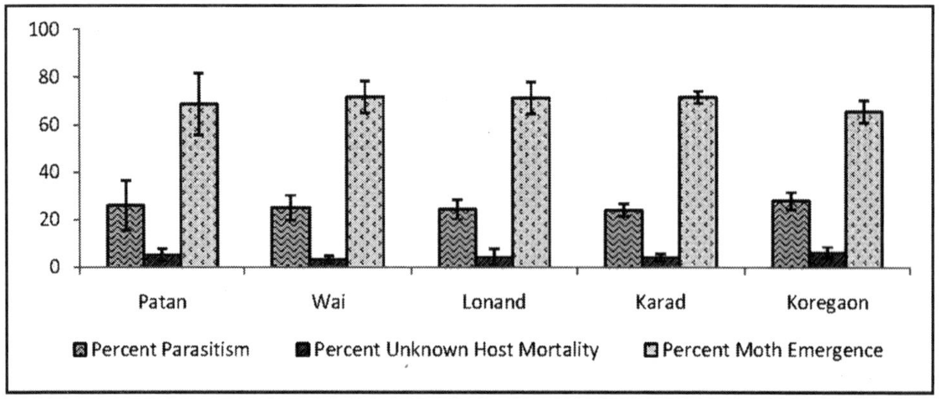

Field efficacy of *X. pedator* of Satara region for 2012-13

Discussion

The field efficacy studies have been carried out by several workers, Battisti (1989), conducted the field study of two hymenopterous parasitoids *Tetrastichus servadeii* Domenichini (Eulophidae) and *Ooencyrtus pityocampae* Mercet (Encyrtidae). Parasitoids efficiently control the pest *Thaumetopoea pityocampa* (Denis and Schiffermiiller) which associated with Australian pine *Pinus nigra* Arnold. He conducted the field efficacy by collection and quantitative observations by collecting the host species from the field, similar attempts has been made to evaluate field efficacy. At international scenario Ellers *et al.* (1998), conducted field efficacy study along with size-fitness relationship in the parasitoid *Asobara tabida* (Hymenoptera: Braconidae) which acts as solitary larval endoparasitoid of *Drosophila*. Similarly Gerling *et al.* (2001), reviewed the results of field efficacy of white fly *Bemisia tabaci* with biological control by using parasitoids and predators. Leppala and King (1996) focused on the production of biocontrol agents for their use in controlling pests of field crops.

Bogran *et al.* (2002) conducted field experiment to analyse the interspecific competition among parasitoids of whiteflies. They found hymenopterous parasitoids like: *Encarsia pergandiella* Howard, *Eretmocerus mundus* Mercet, and *Encarsia formosa* Gahan have potent role in controlling silverleaf whitefly *Bemisia argentifolii* Bellows. Menten (2011), studied use of a cocktail parasitoids against aphids in strawberries and after three years of testing in the laboratory and two years of large scale field trials in Belgium, he developed an efficient method for aphid control.

Ahmad *et al.* (2012), studied potential of egg parasitoid *Trichogramma chilonis* (Ishii) (Hymenoptera: Trichogrammatidae) against the sugarcane stem borer, *Chilo infuscatellus* (Lepidoptera; Pyralidae) under field conditions. They reported the role of *T. chilonis* as a pest management tool for the control of *C. infuscatellus* under natural field conditions by using *Trichogramma* cards in the field of sugarcane. Abd-Rabou (2011), recorded field efficacy of parasitoid, *Coccophagus scutellaris* (Hymenoptera: Aphelinidae) and the predator, *Exochomus flavipes* (Coleoptera: Coccinellidae) against green shield scale *Pulvinaria psidii* (Hemiptera: Coccidae) on guava trees from Egypt. He found the number of parasitized *P. psidii* nymphs by *C. scutellaris* in the studied plots increased from 2 per cent to 54 per cent.

Li *et al.* (2006) conducted field experiments and surveys in 2003 and 2004 to evaluate the efficacy of the parasitoid *Microplitis mediator* (Haliday) to control populations of *Helicoverpa armigera* (Hubner) in cotton fields in Northwestern China's Xinjiang Province. They found that biocontrol agents such as: *M. mediator* caused 80 per cent decrease in cotton boll damage. Teder *et al.* (1999), studied patterns of host use for ichneumon solitary parasitoids with their field evidence from homogeneous habitat. They conducted the field experiment with three ichneumon parasitoids *Exephanes occupator*, *Spilichneum limnophilus* and *Chasmias paludator* against different lepidopteran hosts.

Pucci *et al.* (2003), evaluated field study of parasitism caused by exotic parasitoid *Copidosoma koehleri* on *Phthorimaea operculella* from Central Italy. At Indian scenario Mani *et al.* (2006), studied field efficacy of the introduced parasitoid, *Encarsia guadeloupae* against exotic spiralling whitefly, *Aleurodicus dispersus* in guava. They conducted field trials during 2001 to 2004. After three years they found *E. guadeloupae* was only major natural enemy encountered with parasitism ranged from 78.6 to 98.4 per cent in all the guava orchards.

Sathe (1987b) reported natural enemies of *S. litura* from Kolhapur region, Western India. Agriculturally, it is very sound region with a very high rainfall (700-3000 mm) in Western Maharashtra. *C. chlorideae* caused 60 per cent, mortalities in second stage larvae of *S. litura*. Similarly, *D. argenteopilosa*, *A. prodeniae* and *A. colemani* collectively showed 20 per cent mortality in *S. litura*. Other miner parasitoids he recorded were *Enicospilus* sp. and *Ecthromorpha* causing 5 per cent mortality. Sathe and Chougule (2006) studied natural enemies of *H. armigera* on pigeon pea from Western Maharashtra, India. They reported ten hymenopterous parasitoids and one dipteran tachinid fly, causing mortalities in various pest stages. *C. chlorideae* caused 52 per cent mortalities, *Diadegma fenestralis* Holmgren 13 per cent, *Eriborus trochanteratus* Cameron 7-10 per cent and *Cotesia ruficrus* (Haliday) 7-10 per cent mortalities in the larvae of *H. armigera*, *Trichogramma minutum* Riley caused 20-40 per cent mortalities in eggs of *H. armigera*. Sathe (1984) studied seasonal mortalities in *C. orientalis*, a larval parasitoid of *E. atomosa* from Western Maharashtra, India. Wherein he reported 8.20 per cent, 40.20 per cent and 80.0 per cent mortalities in the months of November, December and January respectively in the cocoons of *C. orientalis* during the years 1980-83. Sathe *et al.* (1986) studied parasitic complex associated with *Chapra mathias* Fab. from paddy ecosystem of Kolhapur region, Western Maharashtra, India. They reported that *Apanteles baoris* W. appeared 15 days after occurrence of pest and caused 5 per cent mortality at beginning but later, reached 87 per cent. Recently, Sathe and Chougule (2014) studied hymenopterous biopesticides and their preliminary biocontrol potential from Western Maharashtra including Ghats they reported 96 hymenoperous parasitoids causing higher mortalities in various pest species.

Summary and Conclusion

Modern agriculture requires awareness towards scientific knowledge and information regarding agricultural crops and their pests with control measures, for increase in the production of agricultural commodities. Cereals, pulses, fruits, vegetables, oilseeds, and plantation crops etc., are the major groups of crops cultivated in India as well as Maharashtra (Singh and Sandhu, 1986). Cereals and horticultural crops have significant importance in Indian agriculture. The major cereal crops cultivated in India are rice, sorghum, maize, wheat, bajra and ragi. Cereals are known as staple foods as they are important part of Indian diet. Agricultural and horticultural crops form an important part of total export of goods to foreign country to earn more foreign exchange. Agricultural and horticultural crops are severely infested with many pests due to which the yield of commodities was adversely affected. Pest damages crop plants by feeding on leaves, stem, inflorescence, fruits, roots etc., and reduces yield. About 35 per cent annual crop losses have been noticed due to damage by pests to crop plants (Sathe, 2009). The development of hybrid varieties enhanced the pest populations leading to pest resistance, pest resurgence, secondary pest outbreak, pesticide residue etc. Besides chemical control, several other control strategies like: cultural control, mechanical control, physical control, radiation control, behavioural control, hormonal control, biological control etc., are the major constituents of IPM programme. Chemical control shows quick knockdown effect as compare to all these but causing various problems such, it may also show negative impact on biocontrol agents like parasitoids and predators also on pollinating agents like honeybees. The biological control primarily works to control the pests, although the process is slow but it gives permanent control of pest. Furthermore, it is almost hazardless, eco-friendly and economical method of pest control. Hence biological pest control is the need of the day.

The parasitoid pest models as: *A. bosei* with *A. moorei*, *G. spodopterae* with *S. litura* and *X. pedator* with *C. partellus* have been studied in the book.

The book has been divided into eight chapters.

The first chapter comprises of Introduction of the topic. The second chapter includes the review of literature. The third chapter devoted to collection, preservation and rearing of biocontrol agents and pests.

The fourth chapter deals with the biology of hymenopterous parasitoids. Biology studied carried with lifecycle of *A. bosei*, *G. spodopterae* and *X. pedator* the average lifecycle of parasitoids were completed in 15.87, 20.97 and 30.40 days respectively.

The average adult longevity was 9.8, 9.2 and 15.2 days for males and 12.6, 10.4 and 18.4 days for females with 50 per cent honey in *A. bosei*, *G. spodopterae* and *X. predator* respectively.

Behavioural studies like: mating and oviposition behaviours of three parasitoids were conducted. For all three parasitoids, mating behaviour consists a series of activities from attraction, recognition, orientation, wing vibration, antennation, mounting, copulation to post copulation grooming. Similarly, for oviposition behaviour all parasitoids showed series of actions like: attraction towards host, recognition, examination of host through antennae, up and down movement of abdomen, ovipositor thrusting and insertion, finally actual oviposition in host body.

The fifth chapter is devoted to reproductive potential of parasitoids. The parasitism was studied on the basis of pest density, pest age and pest specificity. The optimum pest density for getting maximum progeny production was 30 for *X. pedator* and *A. bosei* whereas, 20 for *G. spodopterae.* The optimum pest age for maximum parasitism was 6, 4 and 3 day old host for *A. bosei*, *G. spodopterae* and *X. pedator* respectively. The pest specificity have been analysed to recognize the appropriate host for better improvement of biocontrol potential of parasitoids.

The sixth chapter is devoted to field efficacy of parasitoids. The efficacy have been analysed by per cent parasitism in the field.

The seventh chapter comprises the summary and conclusion and eight for bibliography.

Conclusion

Species diversity of hymenopteran parasitoids has been reported from various agroecosystems of Kolhapur, Sangli and Satara region in which, family Braconidae was dominated, followed by Ichneumonidae. It was found that hymenopteran parasitoids are densely scattered all over in study area and acts as potent biocontrol agents of agricultural pests.

Parasitoid species selected for the experimental studies are: *Apanteles bosei* Bhatnagar (Braconidae), a parasitoid of red hairy caterpillar *Amsacta moorei* (Butler); *Glyptapanteles spodopterae* Ahmad (Braconidae), a parasitoid of leaf eating caterpillar *Spodoptera litura* (Fabricius) and *Xanthopimpla pedator* Fabricius (Ichneumonidae), a parasitoid of lepidopteran stem borer *Chilo partellus* (Swinhoe).

Behavioural studies of parasitoids were conducted under laboratory conditions (25±2°C temperature, 62±5 per cent R.H., and 12 hr photoperiod). All 3 parasitoid species successfully mated and oviposited in the laboratory. The average life cycle of *A. bosei*, *G. spodopterae* and *X. pedator* were completed in 15.87, 20.97 and 30.40 days respectively whereas, average adult longevity of females with 50 per cent honey was 12.6, 10.4 and 18.4 days respectively. The optimum host age for maximum progeny production were 6, 4 and 3 days old hosts of *A. bosei*, *G. spodopterae* and *X. pedator* respectively while, optimum host density were 30 for *A. bosei* and *X. pedator* while, 20 for *G. spodopterae*.

Field efficacy studies were conducted in different field locations of study area and checked the natural parasitism for control of pest species and also evaluated the species richness of parasitoids from study areas. Field efficacy can be conducted with *A. bosei* against *A. moorei*, *G. spodopterae* against *S. litura* and *X. pedator* against *C. partellus*. From the results, we found that all three parasitoids were successfully established in the study area. Comparatively, maximum parasitism of *A. bosei* and *G. spodopterae* were found in Kolhapur region however, maximum parasitism of *X. pedator* was noticed in Sangli region. Interestingly, once parasitoid established in the field it controlled the pest population very effectively.

From above results it is concluded that the parasitoids *A. bosei*, *G. spodopterae* and *X. pedator* possesses enormous parasitism potential against different pests of agricultural importance like: hairy caterpillars, leaf eating caterpillars and lepidopteran stem borers respectively. *A. bosei* showed gregarious nature while *X. pedator* and *G. spodopterae* parasitoids are found to be solitary in nature. However, *A. bosei*, *G. spodopterae* and *X. pedator* found to be effective biocontrol agents of insect pests.

Bibliography

Abd-Rabou, S. (2011). Field Efficacy of Parasitoid, *Coccophagus scutellaris* (Hymenoptera : Aphelinidae) and the Predator, *Exochomus flavipes* (Coleoptera : Coccinellidae) against *Pulvinaria psidii* (Hemiptera : Coccidae) in Egypt. *Journal of Biological Control*, 25(2): 85-91.

Ahmad, A. and Ghulamullah. (1941). Ecological Studies on the Spotted Bollworms of Cotton and their Parasites. II. The Fecundity and Longevity of *Earias fabia* and its Parasites *Microbracon greeni lefroyi* under different Conditions of Temperature and Humidity. *Indian Journal of Ent*omology, 3: 245-284.

Ahmad, S., Ashfaq, M., Hassan, M. and Sahi S.T. (2012). Potential of Parasitoid *Trichogramma chilonis* (Ishii) (Hymenoptera : Trichogrammatidae) against the Sugarcane Stem Borer, *Chilo infuscatellus* (Lepidoptera : Pyralidae) under Field Conditions. *International Journal of Biodiversity and Conservation*, 4(1): 36-38.

Assem van den, J. (1986). Mating Behaviour in Parasitic Wasps. 'Insect Parasitoids', Academic Press, London. pp. 137-167.

Atkins, M.D. (1980). Introduction to Insect Behaviour. Macmillan Publishing Co., Inc. New York. pp. 1-231.

Atwal, A.S. and Dhaliwal G.S. (2002). Agricultural Pests of South Asia and their Management. Kalyani Publishers, New Delhi. pp. 1-498.

Ayyar, P.N.K. and Narayanaswami, P.S. (1940). On the Biology of *Spathius vumeficus* Wilk. A Possible Effective Parasite of *Pempheres affinis* in South India. *Indian Journal of Ent*omology, 3: 245-284.

Azuma, Kan-Ichi and Hideo Kitano. (1971). Experimental Studies on the Parasitism of *Apanteies glomeratus* Linn. on the larvae of *Pieris melete* Menetries. *Kontyu,* 39: 394-399.

Baaren, J.V. and Boivin G. (1998). Genotypic and kin discrimination in a Solitary Hymenopterous Parasitoid: Implications for Speciation. *Evolutionary Ecology,* 12: 523-534.

Barlett, B.R. (1953). A Tactile Ovipositional Stimulus to Culture *Macrocentrus ancylivorus* on An Unnatural Host. *Journal of Economic Entomology,* 46: 525.

Barnes, R.D., Jarvis, R.F., Schweppenhauser, M.A. and Mullin, L.J. (1976). Introduction, Spread and Control of the Pine Woolly aphid, *Pineus pini* (L.), in Rhodesia. *Suid Afrikaanse Bosboutydskrif,* 96: 1-11.

Bastock, M. (1967). 'Courtship, A Zoological Study'. Heinemann Educational, London.

Battaglia D., Isidoro N., Romani R., Bin F. and Pennacchio F. (2002). Mating Behaviour of *Aphidius ervi* (Hymenoptera : Braconidae): The Role of Antennae. *European Journal of Entomology,* 99: 451-456.

Battisti A. (1989). Field Studies on the Behaviour of Two Egg Parasitoid of the Pine Processionary Moth *Thaumetopoea pityocampa. Entomophaga,* 34(1): 29-38.

Beirne, B.P. (1962). Trends in Applied Biological Control of Insects. *Annual Review of Entomology,* 7: 387-400.

Benelli G., Bonsignori G., Stefanini C., and Canale A. (2012). Courtship and Mating Behaviour in the Fruit Fly Parasitoid *Psyttalia concolor* (Szepligeti) (Hymenoptera : Braconidae): The Role of Wing Fanning. *Journal of Pest Science,* 85: 55-63.

Beukeboom, L.W. and Van den Assem J. (2001). Courtship and Mating Behaviour of Interspecific *Nasonia* hybrids (Hymenoptera, Pteromalidae): A Grandfather Effect. *Behaviour Genetics,* 31(2): 167-177.

Beyarslan A. and Aydogdu M. (2013). Additions to the Rare Species of Braconidae Fauna (Hymenoptera : Braconidae) from Turkey. *Munis Entomology and Zoology,* 8(1): 369-372.

Biliotti, E. and Daumal J. (1969). Biology de *Phanerotoma flavitestacea* Fischer (Hymenoptera : Braconidae) Mise Au Point Dven Elevage permanent En. Ven. De. la lutte Biologique, Contre, *Ectomyelois cerataniae* Zel. *Annales de Zoologie Ecologie Animale,* 1: 379-394.

Bogran C.E., Heinz K.M., and Ciomperlik M.A. (2002). Interspecific Competition among Insect Parasitoids: Field Experiments with Whiteflies as Hosts in Cotton. *Ecology,* 83(3): 653-668.

Borgia, G. (1979). Sexual Selection and Evaluation of Mating Systems. Sexual Selection and Reproductive Competition in Insects (M.S. Blum, eds.) Academic Press, New York, pp. 19-80.

Bousch, G.M. and Baerwald, R.A. (1967). Courtship Behaviour and Evidence for a Sex pheromone in the Apple Maggot Parasite *Ophius alloecus. Annals of the Entomological Society of America,* 60: 865-866.

Broodryk, S.W. (1969). The Biology of *Chelonus (Microchelonus) curvimaculatus* Cameron (Hymenoptera : Braconidae). *Journal of the Entomological Society of South Africa,* 32: 169-189.

Calkins, O.O. and Suttar G.R. (1976). *Apannteles millitaris* (Hymenoptera : Braconidae) Biology and Rearing. *Environmental Entomology,* 5: 147-150.

Calvert, D. (1973). Experimental Host Preferences of *Monoctonus paulensis* Including a Hypothetical Scheme of Host Selection. *Annals of the Entomological Society of America,* 66: 28-33.

Canas, L.A. and Robert J.O. (1998). Application of Sugar Solutions to Maize, and the Impact of Natural Enemies on Fall Armyworm. *International Journal of Pest Management,* 44: 59-64.

Cardona, C. and Oatman, E.R. (1971). Biology of *Apanteles dignus* (Hymenoptera : Braconidae), A Primary Parasite of the Tomato pin worm. *Annals of the Entomological Society of America,* 5: 996-1007.

Cherian, C. and Narayanswami. (1942). The Biology of *Microbracon chilonis* Viereck, A Larval Parasite of *Chilo zonellus* (Swin.). *Indian Journal of Entomology,* 4: 1-4.

Cole, L.R. (1970). Observations on the Finding of Mates by Main *Phaeogenes ivisor* and *Apanteles medicanginis. Animal Behaviour,* 18: 184-189.

Coppel, H.C. and Martin J.W. (1977). Biological Insect Pests Suppression. *Advance Series of Agricultural Sciences.* Spinger-Verlag, Berlin Heidenberg, New York, pp. 1-30.

DeBach Paul. (1964). Biological Control of Insect Pests and Weeds. Chapman and Hall Ltd., New Petter Lane, Lond. pp. 1-843.

Directorate of Economics and Statistics. (2001). Economic Survey, Government of Maharashtra. 2000-01.

Doutt, R.L. (1947). Polyendryony in *Copidosoma sp.* Blanchard. *The American Naturalist,* 81: 435-453.

Dowell, R.V. and Horn. D.J. (1975). Mating Behaviour of *Bathyplectes curculionis* (Hym : Ichneumonidae), A Parasitoid of the Alfalfa weevil, *Hypera postica* (Col.: Curculionidae). *Entomophaga,* 20: 271-273.

Drooz, A.T. and Fedde, V.H. (1972). Discriminate Host Selection by *Monodontomerus dentipes, Environmental Entomology,* 1: 522-23.

Dung, D.T., Phuong L.T.H. and Long K.D. (2011). Insect Parasitoid Composition on Soybean, some Eco-biological Characteristics of the Parasitoid, *Xanthopimpla punctata* Fabricius on Soybean leaffolder *Omiodes indicata* (Fabricius) in Hanoi, Vietnam. *Journal of International Society for Southeast Asian Agricultural Sciences*, 17(2): 58-69.

Ellers, J., Jacques, J., Van Alphen, M. and Sevenster, J.G. (1998). A Field Study of Size-fitness Relationships in the Parasitoid *Asobara tabida*. *Journal of Animal Ecology*, 67: 318-324.

FAO Food and Nutrition Series, No. 27, (2013). Sorghum and Millets in Human Nutrition. Food and Agriculture Organiation, David Lubin Memorial Library Cataloguing in Publication, FAO, Rome (Italy). pp. 1-103.

Fincke, O. M., L. Higgins and Rojas, E. (1990). Parasitism of *Nephila clavipes* (Araneae, Tetragnathidae) by An Ichneumonid (Hymenoptera, Polyspinctini) in Panama. *Journal of Arachnology*, 18: 321-329.

Fink, D.E. (1926). The Biology of *Macrocentrus imvora* Rohwer, An Important Parasite of the Strawberry Leaf Roller (*Anylis comptana* Froehl.). *Journal of Agricultural Research*, 32: 1121-1134.

Fisher, S. (1965). Insect Parasitism and Biological Control. *Science Progress*, 53: 567-581.

Gangarde, G.A. (1964). On the Biology of *Campoletis perdistinctus* (Hymenoptera, Ichneumonidae) in Madhya Pradesh. *Annals of the Entomological Society of America*, 57: 570-574.

Genieyes, P. (1925). *Habrobracon brevicornis* Wesm. *Annals of the Entomological Society of America*, 18: 143-202.

Gerling, D., Alomar, O., Arno J. (2001). Biological Control of *Bemisia tabaci* using Predators and Parasitoids. *Crop Protection*, 20: 779-799.

Gordon H.O. (1962). Natural Selection and Ecological Theory. *The American Naturalist*, 96(890): 257-263.

Goswami, V., Khan, M.S. and Srivastava P. (2013). Efficacy and Persistence of Essential Oils and Formic Acid against *Varroa* Mite, *Varroa destructor* in *Apis mellifera* Linn. Colonies. *Agriculture for Sustainable Development*, 1(1): 17-19.

Gupta, V.K. (1987). The Ichneumonidae of the Indo-Australian area (Hymenoptera). Memories of the American Entomological Institutes, 41(1): 1-597.

Hafeez, M. (1961). Seasonal Fluctuation of Population Density of the Cabbage aphid, *Brevicoryne brassicae* (L.) in the Netherlands and the Role of its Parasite, *Aphide* (*Diaeretiella*) *rapae* (Cumts.). *Tijdschrift Over Plantenziekten*, 67: 445-548.

Hallemichael, Y., Smith, J.W. and Weidenmann, R.N. (1994). Host-finding Behaviour, Host Acceptance, and Host Suitability of the Parasite *Xanthopimpla stemmator*. *Entomologia Experimentalis et Applloata*, 71: 155-166.

Hamid, A. Samad, K. and Qadri, M.A.H. (1970). Biology of *Brachycoryphus nursei* (Hymenoptera : Ichneumonidae) in Karachi, Pakistan. *Annals of the Entomological Society of America*, 62: 1382-1385.

Harbo, J.R. and Karft, K.J. (1969). A Study of *Phanerotoma toreutae*, A Parasite of the Pine cone Moth *Laspeyresia torenta*. *Annals of the Entomological Society of America*, 62: 214-20.

Harvey, J.A., van Dam, N.M. and Gols, R. (2003). Interactions over Four Trophic Levels: Foodplant Quality Affects Development of a Hyperparasitoid as Mediated Through a Herbivore and its Primary Parasitoid. *Journal of Animal Ecology*, 72: 520-531.

Hawkins, B.A. (1990). Global Patterns of Parasitoid Assemblage size. *Journal of Animal Ecology*, 59: 57-72.

Hawkins, B.A. and Mills N.J. (1996). Variability in Parasitoid Community Structure. *Journal of Animal Ecology*, 65: 501-516.

Herrebout, W.M. (1969). Some Aspects of Host Selection in *Eucarcelia rutilla* Vill. (Diptera : Tachinidae). *Netherlands Journal of Zoology*, 19: 1-104.

Hidaka, T. (1965). Studies on the Natural Enemies of Insect Injurious to Rice Plant in Tohhoku in Japan District (i) on the Parasite and Predators Attacking the Stem Borer and their Ecological Peculiarities. *Bulletin of Tohoku National Agricultural Experimental Station*, 32: 145-160.

Hopper, K.R. and King. E.G. (1984). Preference of *Microplitis croceipes* (Hymenoptera : Braconidae) for Instars and Species for *Heliothis* (Lepidoptera : Noctuidae). *Environmental Entomology*, 13: 1145-1150.

House, H.L. (1977). In Biological Control by Augmentation of Natural enemies-ed. B.L. Ridgway S-B. Vinson, pp. 150-182.

Idris, A.B. and Hainidh J. (2003). Diversity of Ichneumonid Wasps in the Logged over Forests of Langat Basin in Selangor, Malaysaia. *Journal of Biological Sciences*, 3(2): 259-270.

Jackson, D.J. (1978). The Biology of *Dinocampus* (*Perlitus*) *rutilus* Nees, a Braconid Parasite of *Sitona lineata* L. *Proceedings of the Zoological Society of London*, 2: 597-630.

Jackson, C.G., Neemann, E.G. and Patana, R. (1979). Parasitization of 6 Lepidopteran Cotton Pests by *Chelonus blackburni* (Hym : Braconidae). *Entomophaga*, 24: 99-105.

Kajita, H. and Drake, E.F. (1969). Biology of *Apanteles chilonis* and *Apanteles flavipes*, Parasites of *Chilo suppressalis*. *Mushi.*, 42: 163-74.

Khan, N and Verma, P.M. (1945). Studies on *Erias spp.* the Spotted Bollworms of Cotton in the Punjab Part III. The Biology of Common Parasites of *E. fabia* Stoll, *E. insulana* Boised and *E. cupresvirids* Walker. *Indian Journal of Entomology*, 7: 41-63.

King, B.H. (1990). Sex Ratio Manipulation by the Parasitoid wasp *Spalangia cameroni* in Response to Host Age: A Test of the Host-size Model. *Evolutionary Ecology*, 4: 149-156.

King, B.H. (1994). How do Female Parasitoid Wasps Assess Host Size during Sex-ratio Manipulation? *Animal Behaviour*, 8: 511-518.

King, P.E. and Radchiffe, N.A. (1969). The Structure and Possible Mode of Functioning of the Female Reproductive System in *Nasonia vitripennis*. *Journal of Zoology (London)*, 157: 319-344.

Laing, D.R. and Caltagirone, L.E. (1969). Biology of *Habrobracon lineatellae*. *Canadian Entomologist*, 101: 135-142.

Leong G.K.L. and Oatman, E.R. (1968). The Biology of *Campoplex haywardi* (Hymenoptera : Ichneumonidae), A Primary Parasite of the Potato Tuber Worm. *Annals of the Entomological Society of America*, 61: 26-36.

Leppala N.C. and King E.G. (1996). The Role of Parasitoid and Predator Production in Technology Transfer of Field Crop Biological Control. *Entomophaga*, 41(3/4): 343-360.

Lewis, W.J. (1970). Study of Species and Instars of Larval *Heliothis* Parasitized by *Microplitis croceipes*. *Journal of Economic Entomology*, 63: 363-365.

Lewis, W.J., and Gross H.R. (1989). Comparative Studies on Field Performance of *Heliothis* Larval Parasitoids *Microplitis croceipes* and *Cardiochiles nigriceps* at varying Densities and Under Selected Host Plant Conditions. *Florida Entomologist*, 72: 6-14.

Li, J., Yan, F., Coudron, T.A., Pan, W., Zhang, X., Liu, X., and Zhang, Q. (2006). Field Release of the Parasitoid *Microplitis mediator* (Hymenoptera : Braconidae) for Control of *Helicoverpa armigera* (Lepidoptera : Noctuidae) in Cotton Fields in Northwestern China's Xinjiang Province. *Environmental Entomology*, 35(3): 694-699.

Lingren, P.D., Guerra, R.J., Nickelsen, J.W. and White, C. (1970). Hosts and Host Age Preference of *Campoletis perdistinctus* (Viereck). *Journal of Economic Entomology*, 63: 518-522.

Lingren, P.D. and Nobel, L.W. (1972). Preference of *Campoletis perdistinctus* for Certain noctuid larvae. *Journal of Economic Entomology*, 65: 104-107.

Lyons, L.A. (1976). Mating Ability in *Neodiprion sertifer* (Hymenoptera : Diprionidae). *Canadian Entomologist*, 1016-1026.

Ma, D.Y., Guo, H.L., Liu, F.Z., Kang, F.Z., Sun, J.G., Wang, T.R., and Wang, J.P. (2000). Use *Trichogramma pintoi* to Control *Helicoverpa armigera* in Xinjiang. Chin. *Journal of Biological Control,* 16: 143.

Mani M., Dinesh M.S., Hosetti B.B., Krishnamoorthy A. and Lakshmi P.S.R. (2006). Field Efficacy of the Introduced Parasitoid, *Encarsia guadeloupae* against Exotic Spiralling Whitefly, *Aleurodicus dispersus* in guava. *Indian Journal of Plant Protection,* 34(1): 22-25.

Mason, W.R.M. (1986). Standard Drawing Conventions and Definitions for Venational and other Features of wings of Hymenoptera. *Proceedings of the Entomological Society of Washington,* 88: 1-7.

Mathews R.W. (1974). Biology of Braconidae. *A. Rev. entomol.* 19: 15-32.

Menten, N. (2011). Fresa Protect: The use of a Cocktail of Parasitoids against Aphids in Strawberries - A Case Study. *Integrated Plant Protection in Soft Fruits IOBC/wprs Bulletin,* 70: 217-223.

Mertins, J.W. (1971). Aspects of Sex Attraction in the Introduction Pine Saw Fly, *Diprion Similis* (Hartig) (Hymenoptera : Diprionidae). Ph.D. Thesis, University of Wisconsin.

Nechols, J.R., and Kikuchi, R.S. (1985). Host Selection of the Spherical mealybug (Homoptera : Pseudococcidae) by *Anagyrus indicus* (Hymenoptera : Encyrtidae): Influence of Host Stage on Parasitoid oviposition, Development, Sex Ratio, and Survival. *Environmental Entomology,* 14: 32-37.

Nikam, P.K. and Basarkar, C.D. (1981). Influence of Host Density on Reproductive Potential of *Campoletis chlorideae* (Uchida) (Hymenoptera : Ichneumonidae), An Internal Parasite of *Heliothis armigera* (Hubn.). *Bioresearch,* 5: 101-104.

Nishida T. (1956). An Experimental Study of the Ovipositional Behaviour of *Opius fletcheri* Silvestri, A Parasite of the Melon Fly. *Proceedings of Hawaii Enyomological Society,* 16: 126-34.

Nobel, L.W. and Graham, H.M. (1966). Behaviour of *Campoletis perdistinctus* (Viereck) as a Parasite of the Tobacco Budworm. *Journal of Economic Entomology,* 59: 1118-1120.

Oatman, E.R. Platner, G.R. and Greany, P.D. (1969). The Biology of *Orgillus lepidus* (Hymenoptera : Ichneumonidae), A Primary Parasite of the Potato Tuberworm. *Annals of the Entomological Society of America,* 62: 1407-1414.

Oatman, E.R. and Platner, G.R. (1974). The Biology of *Temelucha* sp., *Platensis* group. (Hymenoptera : Ichneumonidae), A Primary Parasite of the Potato Tuberworm. *Annals of the Entomological Society of America,* 67: 275-280.

Odebiyi, J.A. and Oatman, E.R. (1972). Biology of *Agathis gibbosa* (Hymenoptera : Braconidae), A Primary Parasite of the Potato Tuberworm. *Annals of the Entomological Society of America*, 65: 1104-1114.

Onagbola, E.O., Fadamiro, H.Y. and Mbata G.N. (2007). Longevity, Fecundity, and Progeny Sex Ratio of *Pteromalus cerealellae* in Relation to Diet, Host Provision, and Mating. *Biological Control*, 40: 222-229.

Paroda, R.S. (1993). Crop Science Research for Sustainable Agriculture in India. *Proceedings of the National Academy of Sciences, India*, 63: 97-114.

Pierce, N.E., and Elgar, M.A. (1985). The Influence of Ants on Host Plant Selection by *Jalmenus evagoras*, A Myrmecophilous lycaenid Butterfly. *Behavioural Ecology and Sociobiology*, 16: 209-222.

Polis, G.A. (1991). Complex Trophic Interactions in Deserts: An Empirical Critique of Food-web Theory. *The American Naturalist*, 138: 123-155.

Polis, G.A., and Strong D.R. (1996). Food Web Complexity and Community Dynamics. *The American Naturalist*, 147: 813-846.

Price, P.W. (1971). Niche Breath and Dominance of Parasitic Insects Sharing the same Host Species. *Ecology*, 52: 587-596.

Pucci, C., Spanedda, A.F. and Minutoli, E. (2003). Field Study of Parasitism Caused by Endemic Parasitoids and by the Exotic Parasitoid *Copidosoma koehleri* on *Phthorimaea operculella* in Central Italy. *Bulletin of Insectology* 56 (2): 221-224.

Quedanu, F.W. and Guevermont, H. (1975). Observations on Mating and Oviposition Behaviour of *Priopoda nigricollis* (Hymenoptera : Ichneumonidae), A Parasite of Brich Leaf Miner, *Fenusa pusilla* (Hymenoptera : Tenthredinidae). *Canadian Entomologist*, 107: 1199-1204.

Rabinovich, J.E. (1970). Population Dynamics of *Telenomus fariai* (Hymenoptera : Scelionidae), A Parasite of Chagas, Disease Vectors. II. Effect of host-egg age. *Journal of Medical Entomology*, 7: 477-481.

Raulston, J.R., Graham, H.M., Lingren, P.D., and Snow, J.W. (1976). Mating Interaction of Native and Laboratory Reared Tobacco Budworms Released in the Field. *Environmental Entomology*, 834-839.

Romani, R., Rosi, M.C., Isidoro, N., and Bin, F. (2008). The Role of Antennae during Courtship Behaviour in the Parasitic Wasp *Trichopria drosophilae*. *The Journal of Experimental Biology*, 211: 2486-2491.

Salt, G. (1935a). Experimental Studies in Insect Parasitism. III-Host Selection. *Proceedings of the Royal Society of London Series B-Biological Sciences*, 117: 415-435.

Salt, G. (1935b). Experimental Studies in Insect Parasitization V. The Sense used by *Trichogramma* to Distinguish between Parasitized and Non-parasitized Host. *Proceedings of the Royal Society of London Series B-Biological Sciences*, 122: 57-75.

Sarkar, A., Suasa-ard, W. and Uraichuen, S. (2013). Host Stage Preference and Suitability of *Allotropa suasaardi* Sarkar and Polaszek (Hymenoptera: Platygasteridae), A Newly Identified Parasitoid of Pink Cassava Mealybug, *Phenacoccus manihoti* (Homoptera : Pseudococcidae). *Songklanakarin Journal of Science and Technology*, 37(4): 381-387.

Sathe, T.V. (1984a). Influence of Host Density on the Reproductive Potential of *Cotesia orentalis* Chalikwar and Nikam (Hymenoptera : Braconidae), An Internal Larval Parasitoid of *Exelastis atomosa* Wals. (Lepidoptera : Pterophoridae). *Journal of Scientific Research*, 6(3): 155-156.

Sathe, T.V. (1984b). Reproductive Potential of *Cotesia diurnii* Rao and Nikam (Hymenoptera : Braconidae), A Larval Parasitoid of *Exelastis atomosa* Fab. in Relation to Host Density. *Science and Culture*, 50: 361-362.

Sathe, T.V. (1985). Adult Longevity of *Cotesia diurnii* Rao and Nikam (Hymenoptera : Braconidae) with different Food. *Science and Culture*, 51: 168-169.

Sathe, T.V. (1986a). Life Table and Intrinsic Rate of *Cotesia diurnii* Rao and Nikam (Hymenoptera : Braconidae), A Larval Parasitoid of *Exelastis atomosa* Wals. *Entomon*, 11: 281-283.

Sathe, T.V. (1986b). New Records of Natural Enemies of *Exelastis atomosa* Walsingham, A Pigeon Pea Pest in Kolhapur, India. *Oikoassay*, 3(1): 17.

Sathe, T.V. (1987). Life Table and Intrinsic Rate of Increase of *Diadegma trichoptilus* (Cameron) (Hymenoptera : Ichneumonidae) Population on *Exelastis atomosa* Wals. (Lepidoptera : Pterophoridae). *Journal of Advanced Zoology*, 8(1): 1-4.

Sathe, T.V. (1990). The Biology of *Diadegma argenteopilosa* (Cameron) (Hymenoptera : Ichneumonidae), An Internal Larval Parasitoid of *Spodoptera litura* (Fab.). *The Entomologist* (U.K.) 109: 2-7.

Sathe, T.V. (1991). Fecundity and Life Table Studies in *Glyptapanteles malshri* S and I (Braconidae), A Larval Parasitoid of *Plutella xylostella* (Plutellidae). *Rivista Di Parassitologia*, VIII (LII). N.3, 299-306.

Sathe, T.V. (1993). Host Age Selection by *Apanteles jayanagarensis* Bhatnagar (Hymenoptera : Braconidae), A Parasitoid of *Spilosoma obliqua* (Wlk.). *Comparative Physiology and Ecology*, 18: 140-143.

Sathe, T.V. (2014). Recent Trends in Biological Pest Control pp. 1-190. Astral International Pvt. Ltd., New Delhi.

Sathe, T.V. (2015). Biological Pest Control through Ichneumonids pp. 1-117. Astral International Pvt. Ltd., New Delhi.

Sathe, T.V. and Bhoje, P.M. (1996). Oviposition Behaviour in *Apanteles obliqua* Wilkinson (Hymenoptera), A Parasitoid of *Spilosoma obliqua* (Walk) (Lepidoptera). *J. The Karnataka University Science, (Special Issue),* 1-6.

Sathe, T.V. and Bhoje, P.M. (1998). Host Density Relationship in *Apanteles obliquae,* An Internal Parasitoid of *Spilosoma obliqua. Bulletin of Environmental Sciences (B),* 1: 11-12.

Sathe, T.V. and Bhosale, Y.A. (1996). Impact of *Apanteles creatonoti* (Hymenoptera : Braconidae) on the Population of *Spilosoma oblique. The Madras agricultural journal,* 83: 251-254.

Sathe, T.V. and Bhosale, A.M. (2011). *Plutella xylostella* (L.) density Requirement for Maximum Progeny Production of *Diadegma insulare* (Cameron). *Asian Journal of Animal Sciences,* 6(2): 212-214.

Sathe, T.V. and Chougule, T.M. (2006). Natural Enemies of *Helicoverpa armigera* (Hubn.) on Pigeon Pea from Western Maharashtra. *Indian Journal of Environment and Ecoplanning,* 12(3): 657-659.

Sathe, T.V. and Chougule, T.M. (2014). Hymenopterous Biopesticides and their Preliminary Biocontrol Potential from Western Maharashtra including Ghats. *Biolife,* 2(4): 1254-1261.

Sathe, T.V., Gosawi N.B. and Devgire, D.V. (1986). Parasite Complex Associated with *Chapra mathias* Fab., A Paddy Pest in Kolhapur. *Geobios New Reports,* 5: 59-60.

Sathe, T.V. and Ingawale, D.M. (1993a). Host Age Selection by *Apanteles blateatae* (Hymenoptera : Braconidae), A Parasitoid of *Sylepta derogate. Trends in Life Sciences* (India), 8: 113-116.

Sathe, T.V. and Jadhav, A.D. (2001). Host Plant Attractivity in a Model, *Cotesia glomeratus. Bombyx mori* - Mulberry. *Sericologia,* 41(3): 1-12.

Sathe, T.V. and Margaj, G.S. (1996). Mating Behaviour in *Eriborus argenteopilosus* (Cameron), A Parasitoid of *Heliothis armigera* (Hubn.). *Journal of the Karnataka University Science Special Issue,* 17-21.

Sathe, T.V. and Margaj G.S. (2001). Cotton Pests and Biocontrol Agents. Daya Publishing House, Delhi. pp. 1-166.

Sathe, T.V. and Nikam, P.K. (1983). Mating, Oviposition and Emergence of *Diadegma trichoptilus* (Cameron) (Hymenoptera : Ichneumonidae), A Larval Parasitoid of *Exelastis atomosa* Walsingham. *Current Science,* 52: 501-502.

Sathe, T.V. and Nikam, P.K. (1984). Mating, Oviposition and Emergence of *Cotesia orientalis* Chalikwar and Nikam (Hymenoptera : Braconidae), An Internal Larval Parasitoid of *Exelastis atomosa* Walsingham. *Comparative Physiology and Ecology,* 9: 231-232.

Sathe, T.V. and Nikam P.K. (1985). Influence of Host Density on Percentage Parasitism by *Didegma trichoptilus* (Cameron), A Larval Parasitoid of *E. atomosa* Wals. *India Journal of Parasitology*, 9: 229-230.

Sathe, T.V. and Shanthakumar, M.V. (1989). Impact of *Diadegma argenteopilosa* Cameron on the population of *Spodoptera litura* (Fab.). *Bulletin of Environmental Sciences*, 7: 7-12.

Sathe, T.V. and Santhakumar, M.V. (1992). Host Specificity in *Campoletis chlorideae* Uchida (Hymenoptera : Ichneumonidae). *Journal of Advanced Zoology*, 13: 53-56.

Sathe, T.V., Santhakumar, M.V. Inamdar, S.A. and Ingawale, D.M. (1987). Reproductive Potential of *Apanteles cratonoti* Viereck (Hym.) in Relation to age of *T. postica* (Wlk.) caterpillar (Lep.). *Uttar Pradesh Journal of Zoology*, 1: 89-91.

Sato, Y. (1975). Rearing *Apanteles glomerotus* L. on the larvae of *Pieris rapae crucivora* Biosduval fed on an artificial diet. *Kontyu* (Tokyo), 43: 242-249.

Sawant S.D., Kulkarni B.N., Achuthan C.V. and Satyasai K.J. (1999). Agricultural Development in Maharashtra Problems and Prospects. Ed. National Bank for Agriculture and Rural Development, Mumbai. pp. 1-185.

Schmidt, G.T. (1974). Host-acceptance Behaviour of *Campoletis sonorensis* towards *Heliothis zea*. *Annals of the Entomological Society of America*, 67: 835-844.

Seitner, M. and Notzl, P. (1925). *Pityophthorus hensdchell* Seitner and Sein Parasit *Cosmophorus henschell* Ruschka. *Zeitschrift für Angewandte Entomologie*, 11: 187-196.

Sih, A., Englund G., and Wooster D. (1998). Emergent Impacts of Multiple Predators on Prey. *Trends in Ecology and Evolution*, 13: 350-355.

Simmonds, F.J. (1963). Genetics and Biological Control Problems. *Entomophaga*, 17: 251-264.

Singh, A., and Sandhu, A.N. (1986). Agricultural Problems in India. Jammu University, Jammu. pp. 386.

Smilowitz, Z. and Iwantsch, G.E. (1975). Relationship between the parasitoid *Hyposoter exigua* and the cabbage looper, *Tricoplusia ni*. The Effect of Host age on Ovipositional Rate of the Parasitoid and Successful Parasitism. *Canadian Entomologist*, 107: 689-694.

Smith, J.M. (1957). Effects of the Food of California Red Scale, *Aonidiella aurantii* (Mask.) on Reproduction of its Hymenopterous Parasites. *Canadian Entomologist*, 89: 219-230.

Somchoudhary, A.K. and Dutt, N. (1988). Influence of Hosts and Host Age on the Bionomics of *Trichogramma perkinsi* Girault and *Trichogramma australicum* Girault. *Indian Journal of Ent*omology, 50: 374-379.

Srivastava, K.P. (1996). A Textbook of Applied Entomology. Kalyani Publishers, New Delhi. pp. 1-321.

Steiner, S.M., Kropf C., Graber W., Nentwig W. and Klopfstein S. (2010). Antennal Courtship and Functional Morphology of Tyloids in the Parasitoid Wasp *Syrphoctonus tarsatorius* (Hymenoptera: Ichneumonidae: Diplazontinae). *Arthropod Structure and Development*, 39(1): 33-40.

Sundaramurthy, V.T. and Chitra, K. (1987). Insect Management in the Cotton System in India. ICAR. pp 1-29.

Tagwa, J. (1984). Diapause in the Braconid Wasps *Apanteles glomeratus* L.(I) Evidence of diapause in Oven Wintering Prepupae. *Applied Entomology and Zoology*, 19: 396-399.

Tawfik, M.F.S. (1975). Host Parasite Specificity in a Braconid *Apanteles glomeratus* L. *Nature*, 179: 1031-1032.

Teder, T., Tammaru, T. and Pedmanson, R. (1999). Patterns of Host use in Solitary Parasitoids (Hymenoptera, Ichneumonidae): Field Evidence from a Homogeneous Habitat. *Ecography*, 22: 79-86.

Thornhill, R. and Alcock, J. (1983). 'The Evalution of Insect Mating Systems'. Harvard University Press, Cambridge, Massachusetts. pp. 1-240.

Thrope, W.H. and Jones, F.G.W. (1937). Olfactory Conditioning in a Parasitic Insect and its Relation to the Problem of Host Selection. *Proceedings of the Royal Society of London Series B-Biological Sciences*, 124: 56-81.

Thurston, R. and Postely, L. (1978). Effect of Instar of *Manduca Sexta* on the Rate of Development of its Parasite, *Apanteles congregatus*. *Tobacco Science*, 22: 33-34.

Tikar, O.T. and Thakare, K.R. (1961). Bionomics, Biology and Immature Stages of an Ichneumonid. *Horogenes fenestralis* Holmgren, A Parasite of Gram Caterpillar. *Indian Journal of Ent*omology, 23: 116-124.

Tilley, L.A.N., Croft, P. and Mayhew, P.J. (2011). Control of a Glasshouse Pest Through the Conservation of Its Natural Enemies? An Evaluation of Apparently Naturally Controlled Shore Fly Populations. *Biological Control*, 56(1): 22-29.

Townes, H. (1969). The Genera of Ichneumonidae, Part 1. Memoirs of the American Entomological Institute, 11: 1-300.

Trimble, R.M. and Wellington, W.G. (1979). Effects of Salinity on Site Selection by Ovipositing *Aedes togoi* (Diptera : Culicidae). *Canadian Journal of Zoology*, 57: 593-596.

Van Alphen, J.J.M. and Janssen, A.R.M. (1982). Host Selection by *Asobara tabida* Nees (Braconidae, Alysiinae), A Larval Parasitoid of Fruit Inhabiting *Drosophila* Species. II. Host Species Selection. *Netherlands Journal of Zoology*, 32: 215-231.

Verma, C.C. and Bindra, O.S. (1974). Laboratory Studies on Host Parasite Relationship to *Apanteles spp.*, When Reared on *Chilo partellus* (Swinhoe). *Indian Journal of Entomology*, 26(2): 110-112.

Vinson, S.B. (1972). Competition and Host Discrimination between Two Species of Tobacco Budworm Parasitoids. *Annals of the Entomological Society of America*, 65: 229-236.

Vinson, S.B. (1975). Biochemical Coevolution between Parasitoids and their Hosts. In *Evolutionary Strategies of Parasitic Insects and Mites*, ed. P.W. Drica, 14-48. New York : Plenum, pp. 1-225.

Wang, X.G., John Duff., Keller M.A., Zalucki M.P., Liu S.S. and Bailey P. (2004). Role of *Diadegma semiclausum* (Hymenoptera: Ichneumonidae) in Controlling *Plutella xylostella* (Lepidoptera: Plutellidae) : Cage Exclusion Experiments and Direct Observation, *Biocontrol Science and Technology*, 14(6): 571-586.

Wang, X.G. and Keller, M.A. (2002). A Comparison of the Host-Searching Efficiency of two Larval Parasitoids of *Plutella xylostella* . *Ecological Entomology*. 27: 104-115.

Wanga, Z.Y., He, K.L., Zhang, F., Lu, X. and Babendreier, D. (2014). Mass Rearing and Release of *Trichogramma* for Biological Control of Insect Pests of Corn in China. *Biological Control*, 68: 136-144.

Weseloh, R.M. (1977). Mating Behaviour of the Gypsy Moth Parasite *Apanteles melanoscelus*. *Annals of the Entomological Society of America*, 70: 549-554.

Weseloh, R.M. (1981). Host Location by Parasitoids. In : *"Semiochemicals, their Role in Pest Control"* (D.A. Nordlund R.L., Jones and W.J. Lewis eds.). pp. 79-95.

West, W.D. (2012). Geology in the Service of India. *Everyman's Science*, XLVI (5), 262-270.

Wilson D.D. and Ridgway R.L. (1975). Morphology, Development, and Behaviour of the Immature Stages of the Parasitoid, *Campoletis sonorensis* (Hymenoptera : Ichneumonidae). *Annals of the Entomological Society of America*, 68(2): 191-196.

Yazdinejad, A.M. and Jussila R. (2009). A Contribution to Ichneumonid Wasps of Iran (Hym.: Ichneumonidae): Anomaloninae, Cremastinae, Ctenopelmatina, Mesochorinae, Metopiinae and Orthopelmatinae. *Applied Entomology and Phytopathology*, 76(2): 11-28.

Zenil, M., Liedo, P., Williams, T., Valle, J., Cancino, J. and Montoya, P. (2004). Reproductive Biology of *Fopius arisanus* (Hymenoptera: Braconidae) on *Ceratitis capitata* and *Anastrepha* spp. (Diptera: Tephritidae). *Biological Control*, 29: 169-178.

Index

*****